PAUL J. STANKARD
Homage to Nature

All art is but imitation of nature.

SENECA (8 BC–65 AD), EPISTLES, I, 65,3

PAUL J. STANKARD
Homage to Nature

by Ulysses Grant Dietz

Photographs by John Bigelow Taylor

HARRY N. ABRAMS, INC., PUBLISHERS

Editor: Ruth A. Peltason
Designer: Ana Rogers

Library of Congress Cataloging-in-Publication Data

Dietz, Ulysses G. (Ulysses Grant), 1955–
Paul Stankard : homage to nature / by Ulysses Grant Dietz ;
photographs by John Bigelow Taylor.
p.   cm.
Includes bibliographical references.
ISBN 0–8109–4473–1 (cloth)
1. Stankard, Paul, 1943–   .   2. Glass art—New Jersey—Mantua—
—History—20th century.   I. Taylor, John Bigelow.   II. Title.
NK5198.S677D54   1996
748.092—dc20   96–10850

Contents

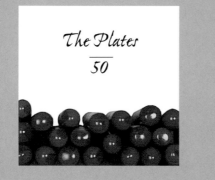
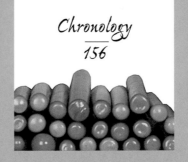
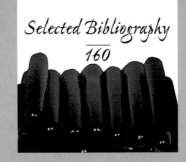

Acknowledgments

$\mathcal{I}$ am deeply honored to author this book on Paul Stankard and his work. I have known Paul since 1984, when I purchased three of his pieces for the permanent collection of The Newark Museum. My training is not in art history, but in the history of material culture and the decorative arts. Thus I bring to this volume my own set of prejudices and my own point of view. The question of whether or not craft objects are art continues to be largely irrelevant to me. Beauty and craftsmanship are valid ends in themselves, as are utility and the upholding of craft traditions. However, having initially admired Paul Stankard's work for its technical virtuosity and its connection with historical glass traditions (particularly those of southern New Jersey), I have come to understand it both as art—Paul's art—and as part of a noble and ancient decorative arts tradition.

I think that without question Paul is the greatest living master of the paperweight maker's art in the world today. He has transcended historical limitations and modern-day prejudices, and he has always remained faithful to his vision. Not all artists can survive the scrutiny of their fans, but knowing Paul simply makes it easier to love his work. He has achieved a rare thing: personal and artistic integrity. What greater joy in life than to be able to say that?

Biographical information on Paul Stankard was obtained both from direct conversations with the artist and from the extensive interview done by Richard Polsky of the Columbia University Oral History Office in August 1990. Robert J. Charleston's *Masterpieces of Glass* was an invaluable source of material on the history and development of glass as was Paul Hollister's article, "Natural Wonders, The Lampwork of Paul J. Stankard," which appeared in the February/March 1987 issue of *American Craft*. I am indebted to Paul and his family for all of their cooperation and support.

ULYSSES GRANT DIETZ
Maplewood, New Jersey
August 1995

Mastering the Flame: The Life and Work of Paul Stankard

To see a world in a grain of sand
And a heaven in a wild flower,
Hold infinity in the palm of your hand
And eternity in an hour.

WILLIAM BLAKE, 1757–1827
"Auguries of Innocence" (c.1803)

A Day in the Studio with Paul It is a typical July day in southern New Jersey: hot, humid, an intermittent breeze serving only to stir up the sun-roasted air. We are gathered, four of us, in Paul Stankard's studio, attached (in lieu of a garage) to Paul and Pat Stankard's home in Mantua, a New Jersey suburb of Philadelphia. The studio is bright and cheerful, its red-painted concrete floor worn from the constant rolling of the wheeled stools. Failed experiments and the work of other glass artists fill dusty shelves in

The bench burner is at the center of Stankard's workbench, along with carbon shaping tools and drawn rods of colored glass in easy reach. The Latin legend on the ventilation hood above, Laborare est Orare, *translates as, To Labor is to Pray.*

front of the various windows. Gardens of wild flowers are visible through every window. The spacious modern, wood-clad house is air-conditioned, alluringly cool. My three hosts refer to it as the observation tank; Patricia Stankard sometimes appears at the glass doors to check on us, holding her dimpled blond grandson Sebastian. We all find it is better not to go into the house unless absolutely necessary, because one does get accustomed to the temperature in the studio, where a single electric fan moves the air. The dim chill of the house only reminds you of the heat, and we all have to remain in the studio for the day, because there is work to be done.

Paul and his two assistants, wearing protective tinted eyeglasses, work at rocket-shaped brass gas/oxygen nozzles (called bench burners), faces close to the big yellow-blue jets of flame. I am their disciple for the day, their rare workday witness, pen and pad poised to help me understand what it is they are doing. The atmosphere is relaxed, chatty, but I suspect the chatter would be absent if not for my presence. Paul shares the long workbench under the window facing the swimming pool with David Graeber, twenty-eight, who has worked as his assistant for six years. Good-looking, with big blue eyes and an easy smile, David is a local boy, raised a few miles away in Woodbury, trained in woodworking. At a smaller workbench, tucked into a corner by the glass doors leading into the house, sits Christine Kressley, twenty-nine, the eldest of Paul and Pat's five children. She has her mother's delicate prettiness and dark blond hair, mingled with her father's unmistakable Irish smile and twinkling blue eyes. Chris grew up in this house, in this studio, and began to work for her father four years ago, after a stint in the nonprofit museum world.

The Stankards' second daughter, Pauline, lives next door with her husband. On the other adjacent lot, a dozen yards distant, is a little green-sided bungalow from the 1920s, which Paul recently acquired and has renovated as his gallery, office, and library. One little bedroom has been turned into a book-lined study, full of volumes on flowers and glass. The other is Christine's office. She also handles correspondence and clerical work for Paul, although he confesses that he'd rather have her using her talent at the bench than spending time on office matters. The basement, which has been painted with a rainbow of bright colors to minimize its dankness, is already in use as an experimental studio, where Paul, Dave, and Chris can explore technical and aesthetic possibilities. Here, too, is stored the bulk glass, the thick foot-long rods of colored glass from Germany and other glass from Italy. The gallery upstairs is devoid of any of Paul's own work. Work by other contemporary glass artists is there, as well as paintings by Paul and Pat's third daughter, Katherine, who is a painter and works in the studio part-time. Someday Paul hopes to add a studio onto this building, extending in the direction of the present house and studio. That way, he tells me sheepishly, they can convert the studio into a garage, which in all these years they've never had.

The artist beside his glass storage case, which is filled with thick rods of raw colored commercial glass. He uses German, Italian, and American glass in his work.

The entire Stankard place feels like an eighteenth-century American master artisan's compound, the comfortable enclave of a modern-day Paul Revere, perhaps. The house, shop, and gallery are all cheek-by-jowl, and his family life is never far distant from his work. For all his renown and the demand for his work, his staff is but two, with practical assistance from his wife. The brick patio, the heated swimming pool, and the big dark-blue Cadillac parked by the carefully landscaped walled garden out front are all icons of comfortable modern suburban life; but they also translate easily into the images of refinement and ease attained by master craftsmen in Colonial New Jersey, before the distinctions between artist and artisan, entrepreneur and laborer, became codified in the nineteenth century. Paul Stankard, master of flameworking and the twentieth-century paperweight, has achieved an eighteenth-century *beau ideal* that Thomas Jefferson would have admired. It is a rare achievement in the craft world, or indeed, in any world.

But what Paul Stankard creates in this artisan's ideal is a far cry from the output of the Colonial South Jersey glassmakers of Wistarburgh or Glassboro—whose daily product used to be carted past Paul's present-day front door on their way to the river. His work has nothing to do with the crimped and mold-blown sugar bowls and whimsies produced by New Jersey's colonial glass gaffers, when at day's end they could cease producing gin bottles and windowpanes. What Paul makes is at once decorative art and art. What he produces is contemplative, awe-inspiring, and spiritual. In this studio, eighteenth- and nineteenth-century glass traditions are fused and transformed into something unique, both in terms of the past and in terms of contemporary studio glass.

Spirituality, of a kind rooted in his Irish Catholic upbringing, but clearly evolved beyond such limitations, is at the core of Paul's work, and this, too, sets him apart from a Colonial artisan. Paul is more like a medieval monk, seated at his desk in a scriptorium in some far-off monastery. He labors on, hour after hour, day after day, illuminating the words of a sacred manuscript. Tiny details are painstakingly drawn in tempera, touched with gold leaf and gesso. Many colors, many minute movements are needed to produce the initial letter for just a single line of scripture. His work is not essential, or at least so it seems. The words would be just as sacred without his efforts. The illumination is unnecessary. Or is it? What does illumination do? It draws the eye, it highlights, it calls attention to that which is holy, that which is, ultimately, important. The worldly eye is caught by the beauty of the illuminator's art. Once caught, it then can turn to the words, the written documentation of God's presence on earth. And so Paul illuminates the physical "words" of God. With his tiny fragments of glass, shaped miraculously into authentic renditions of living wild flowers, he draws the worldly eye to the triumph of his artifice. And in so doing he reminds the viewer of the real miracle, the wild flower itself, which for Paul is the living presence of God.

> *To him who in the love of Nature holds*
> *Communion with her visible forms,*
> *she speaks*
> *A various language.*
>
> WILLIAM CULLEN BRYANT, 1794–1878
> *Thanatopsis* (1817–21)

Growing Up Paul Joseph Stankard was born on April 7, 1943, in North Attleboro, Massachusetts, a longtime center of the electroplated silver industry. Despite the industry, it was a small town of 15,000 people, closely surrounded by woods and dairy farms. His father was a chemist for the Hercules Corporation in nearby Mansfield. Paul was the second of eight children, and the family home was close to what seemed to Paul an endless forest. The focus of Paul's work in glass has its origins in those New England woods, in the wild flowers that grew there. The importance of family in his life came from that crowded, happy Irish Catholic household. Two flora-related family legends from his early childhood remain with him as a sort of premonition of the influence of plants in his life. As an infant, apparently he was inclined to try to eat the leaves off the rubber tree in the living room. His father laughed it off as symptomatic of a vitamin deficiency at the time, but Paul recalls the story as somehow prophetic of his attraction to plants. As a more mobile toddler, he would be put out in the backyard under the watchful eye of his older brother. For the brother, "help" came in the form of an enormous sunflower, which struck terror into Paul's heart. Since the sunflower plant blocked the way out of the backyard, Paul never had the courage to escape to freedom out of fear of passing the sunflower. From his earliest memories, flowers have been powerful symbols for him.

Like many of his peers in the heavily Irish North Attleboro, Paul and his siblings were sent to St. Mary's, a parochial grammar school. While his older brother, Martin, did well, Paul was never a good student. His elementary school years were fraught with struggle and failure because of his inability to read easily. His parents, both college-educated children of the depression, were dismayed. They did everything parents of the fifties could do to improve his academic skills, from bribing him to read (at the rate of a penny a page), to threatening to pull him out of the safety of St. Mary's and throw him to the "Bohemians and monsters" in the public school system. In an era when education was still seen as the only way to self-improvement, and learning disabilities were all but unheard of, Paul's problems were frustrating and traumatic to both him and his parents. Ironically, it was his academic difficulties that ultimately steered Paul to glassblowing and set his path for life.

Having made it through St. Mary's by 1957, Paul went to North Attleboro High for just a year, entering and failing a college preparatory program. Perhaps the only propitious event in that school year was a term paper he wrote for a science class. He chose to write about America's first industry, which, as it happened, was the glass industry of South Jersey. The Stankard family moved down to southern New Jersey, to the town of Wenonah, that year, although Paul has never lost his Massachusetts accent. He completed high school in the flat, sandy farmlands that were home to America's oldest glassblowing industry. There he continued his academic struggles, attending summer school to please his parents and to honor their need to see all their children properly educated.

Throughout his school years, Paul's mother never stopped trying to build up his self-esteem and to encourage him. When his grades slipped, she'd say he was good with his hands and tell him that he could be a dentist, or a gym teacher. She wanted him to have goals and not to give up on himself.

High school efforts aside, Paul was a happy, sociable teenager. He had, as his mother put it, the gift of gab, and was outgoing and popular. Throughout his childhood, perhaps as a release from the burden of books and the struggle of learning, he spent a great deal of time outdoors. He explored the woods and fields near his home, and continued to be influenced by the plants and wild flowers he saw there. He had a paper route, and loved to do other sorts of odd jobs to earn pocket money. His grandfather, who had run a small engraving firm related to the jewelry industry, lived with the Stankards until Paul was fourteen. Taking his grandfather's lead, and probably thanks to some of his genes as well, Paul developed a love of tinkering, of building things and gadgets. He was fond of using found objects, in particular those he unearthed in the bulldozed foundation of a defunct jewelry factory in North Attleboro. It wasn't large-scale equipment that drew him, but small fragments, bits of wire and springs and small pieces of glass jewelry found amidst the rubble of the factory. He would fantasize about building a complicated Rube Goldberg sort of machine, and eventually created one when he was twelve. It didn't do anything in particular, but it satisfied his enjoyment of working with his hands, and let his mind's creativity work untrammeled.

Art was not much of an influence for the Stankard family. Paul's father was trained in chemistry, and his mother had a degree in Latin. Intellectual rigor was important, but art was seen as impractical, even frivolous. Art courses were not encouraged. The only musical instrument that was approved of in the Stankard household was the piano. However, skill in using your hands was useful, and certainly nothing to be ashamed of. So Paul was encouraged in this by both of his parents. Even as a professional with a good salary, Paul's father had a large family to feed, and his values were disciplinarian and utilitarian. Life for a large middle-class household was not as comfortable then as now, and the children were all expected to make their own way in the world. Achievement was the road to independence, and the influence of the depression colored the way the Stankards raised their children.

Accordingly, when Paul squeaked through Pitman High School at the bottom of his class in 1961, he decided to enter the two-year Salem County Vocational Technical Institute (now Salem County Community College). Armed with brochures from his high school guidance counselor, he presented the idea to his father at dinner one evening. His parents, probably none too happy at the thought of four (or more) torturous years trying to get Paul through college, were both pleased at his initiative. Based on the courses taught at Salem, Paul first considered becoming a machinist. Paul's father, pleased at the thought of his son having a good, stable, income-producing trade of which he could be proud, perused the brochure. It was he, rather than Paul, who first latched onto the idea of glass-blowing. Salem, being in the center of the old glass industry of South Jersey, offered the only scientific glassblowing program in the country. To Paul's father it must have seemed to be an answer to his son's search for a career. As a chemist, he knew glassblowers who made glass for laboratories, and he thought it would be a perfect career for Paul. He waxed enthusiastic about the profession, and Paul, startled by his pragmatic father's unwonted excitement, agreed. "OK, I'll be a glassblower," was his response. And that was that.

Dyslexia, the underlying problem that had haunted Paul all his life, lay undiscovered until he was nearly thirty. His sister, Margaret, who was then in college in West Virginia learning special education, was the first person to test his reading. It was she who suggested that Paul might be dyslexic, although it didn't sink in until the early 1970s when he listened to Phil Donahue, on his Chicago-based radio talk show, interview a famous athlete who was dyslexic. For Paul, the past began to make sense. After a lifetime of self-doubt, his academic problems being misconstrued as either stupidity or laziness by his teachers, he finally understood. "I'd never felt I was stupid," he said in an interview in 1990. "It was very refreshing to learn this."

The masterpiece should appear as the flower to the painter — perfect in its bud as in its bloom — with no reason to explain its presence — no mission to fulfill — a joy to the artist, a delusion to the philanthropist — a puzzle to the botanist — an accident of sentiment and alliteration to the literary man.

JAMES MCNEILL WHISTLER, 1834–1903
The Gentle Art of Making Enemies (1890)

Making the Pieces of Nature

The heart and soul of Paul Stankard's work is flameworking, a technique probably dating back to Roman times and earlier. After a long hiatus following the collapse of the Roman Empire, the technique reappeared in the late Middle Ages in France, where its best-known practitioners were located in the central French city of Nevers. It is thought that the earliest Nevers lampworkers may have

DRAWING GLASS
David Graeber heats a chunk cut from a rod of raw glass over a gas/oxygen flame. The heated glass is then pulled, taffylike, into a rod of smaller diameter. When the drawn rods are of a small enough diameter, they are cut, once cool, into workable lengths.

been Italian, as the city was ruled by the dukes of Mantua. (The name of Mantua, New Jersey, does not come from the Italian city, but from an alteration of a Lenape Indian word, *manta,* meaning frog.) Lampworking, as it was originally called, consisted of melting and manipulating small rods and tubes of glass over a lamp flame. The flame was made hot enough to melt the glass by using a foot-powered bellows to concentrate a stream of air on the lamp flames. According to Robert Charleston in his *Masterpieces of Glass,* Nevers was particularly known for its miniature sculptural figures worked in colored glass, but both France and Italy could boast accomplished artisans working at the lamp. Modern-day lampworking is done using pressurized propane gas and oxygen, regulated through bench-mounted torches; hence the term *flameworking* has evolved.

In Paul's studio, the morning's menu offers bits and pieces. Paul, Christine, and David each work at their own bench, at their own flame, to produce the elements that Paul will assemble into a sculptural whole later on in the day. For many years, Paul did all of this alone, gradually developing a repertoire of elements in a way a painter or composer does. These days, having developed and mastered a single element, he may train one of his assistants to produce it, and leave that part of the whole to them. Chris has perfected the bees and damselflies. Dave is the master of blueberries, leaves, and word canes. Throughout the morning, the conversation never stops. Questions, advice, and suggestions go back and forth across the studio, above the constant shimmer of cicadas outside, and the hiss of the flames inside.

Christine is preparing glass for the wings of damselflies, the small, brightly colored insects that flourish in the summer heat. A special amber glass is used for the wings. Paul buys the 1.5"-thick colored glass rods in twenty- or thirty-pound quantities that give him nearly a lifetime supply. Starting with a rod of glass far too thick to work with, Chris has to melt it with the flame and draw the molten glass out into canes of manageable thickness. Depending on what she's making, she might then mix the glass with another color, casing it (giving it a thin layer of a second color) to create depth and a naturalistic effect. The preparation of the material for damselfly wings is time-consuming, and there is an ongoing debate as to how dark the wings should be on the finished insect. The palest amber, with a fine web of black lines applied before the final shape is formed, seems to be the preferred tone. But the wings must not disappear entirely, or be too pale to see; nor can they be too strongly amber. After half the morning has gone by, Paul realizes that Chris has been working with rods of opalescent amber glass—they have an olive tone in reflected light, but are translucent amber in transmitted light. This opalescent glass won't work for the insect wings, because the color is too pink, too unnatural. While Paul doesn't strive for biological perfection in his work, he does always seek to achieve what he calls *organic credibility*. He wants his floral sculptures to seem to be scientifically correct, even though close inspection reveals them to be more impressionistic and stylized than a first glance would suggest. Paul approaches his natural subjects as a painter would, editing for clarity, without losing the visual truth of the plant or insect.

Since Chris's opalescent amber doesn't stand up to Stankard's criterion, she must scrap her morning's work. She resigns herself to this with good cheer, and Paul asks Chris to work instead on another of her specialties for today's paperweight, a honeybee. For many years a living hive of honeybees, constructed by a beekeeper friend, was attached to the studio, so that Paul could study their movements and their shapes. (Ultimately, the heat of the studio drove the bees to abandon their hive.) From this experience, Paul can give a lecture on the life cycle of honeybees. It is the cycle of life, after all, that dominates the content of his work, and he studies it as it hums all around him.

BEE AND YELLOW FLOWER PROCESS *The honeybee is sealed to a preassembled honeycomb section, itself made up of many small hexagonal canes fused together in the oven. A completed coronet blossom is sealed onto the honeycomb.*

David is working on leaves and blueberries for today's paperweight. The blueberries appeared in Paul's botanical vocabulary a few years ago. Their inclusion in his work grew out of vivid recollections of picking wild berries in North Attleboro. His mother would bake fresh blueberry pies for him as a reward for his efforts, and to this day they invoke some the happiest memories of his childhood. As part of the rhythm of nature, the berry represents the ultimate fruition, literally and figuratively, of the plant. These are the final products before the onset of decay and dormancy of winter's temporary death. Pollination, flowering, fruit, decay, rebirth; simple imagery redolent of a Catholic upbringing and a life lived in semirural settings.

As with much of his repertoire, the blueberry required a great deal of experimentation before the correct look could be produced effectively and reliably. A small sphere of

BLUEBERRY PROCESS
A black bead of glass is melted and then dusted or rolled in crushed powder-blue glass. After the tiny black glass sepals are added to the berry, a brown-cased green glass stem is applied and the berry is flame-annealed to stabilize.

black glass is first shaped from a rod of glass. Then the still-hot blob is rolled in powdered violet-blue glass, producing just the right powdery surface and color. Dave rolls the blob to fuse the crushed glass onto the black matrix. Tiny bits of black glass are added to one end of the berry, to produce the little spiky crown of sepals, remnants of the blossom. Finally, a stem of amber glass cased with green is added, and the complete berry is placed on a hot plate to keep it stable for final assembly. The development of the blueberry was not without its hitches. Early on, the constant reheating of the blue surface to apply the details apparently degraded the integrity of the glass, making it incompatible with the molten crystal. The result was internal fractures which would happen in the annealing process, destroying a day's work. The Stankard studio is littered with such failures, each one representing many hours of lost labor. But these failures also represent learning, and once problems are identified, they can be circumvented. Every new flower or form presents new challenges, and every challenge overcome adds a new word to the Stankard vocabulary.

Dave is also making tiny leaves, casing two shades of green glass together for a more natural tone, then drawing and crimping each leaf to produce the ribbed texture of the surface. Paul describes the casing of different colors of glass as like creating colored washes of watercolor, or translucent glazes of oil color on a canvas. The flat, opaque pigments of the German glass are as unnatural as paint from the tube. Dave gives the leaves a final shaping, giving one a curl, while another remains fairly flat, and then onto the hot plate they go, joining neat rows of unassembled elements. Slender corkscrew tendrils, combining green and amber glass, are also on Dave's menu for the morning.

But most fascinating of all at Dave's workbench, and something of which Paul is especially proud, are the word canes that have been appearing in his work for the last few years or so. These began with the little round signature canes that Paul still uses, a PS with a two-digit number to signify the year. Paul began to fashion these in the early 1980s, and it occurred to him that tiny words, all but hidden among the leaves and blossoms and roots of his glass plants, could add a conceptual dimension to his work. All of the words relate to the universal cycle life and growth.

At present the dictionary is limited to five basic words, all spelled out in minute block letters: *seeds, fertile, wet, scent,* and *pollen. Wet* remains Paul's favorite word for the moment, while *pollen* is losing interest for him (not elemental enough, he says). *Terra,* Latin for earth or soil, is a very recent experimental addition, as Paul looks for something of the mystery imposed by the liturgical language of his childhood religion. Originally Paul and his assistants made the canes in-house, but now they are produced to his specifications by a glassmaker in Seattle.

The point of a pencil shows the tiny size of a drawn double word cane reading fertile/seeds.

Essential to his work, but impossibly time-consuming, the word canes are produced in "raw" format. Long thin strips of black glass are carefully arranged and then encased in opaque white glass, with an outer layer of opaque green. When sliced like cold cuts, they produce an oval section with capital letters about one-quarter inch high. The canes themselves are about one inch wide and one-half inch high, perhaps eight inches long. Similar canes were used to date some nineteenth-century French paperweights and were produced in essentially the same way.

David heats the big word canes and repeatedly draws them smaller and smaller. Miraculously, the words do not distort as they are stretched smaller and smaller. When he finally slices off the tiny segments, known by their Italian name, murini, they measure only one-eighth inch high and three-sixteenth inch wide—one-twentieth their original size. Very strong eyes can just make out the words when they're positioned among the roots of a paperweight, but Paul's intent is that you need to use a magnifying glass. A Stankard paperweight is not something to be glanced at, but studied. *Murini* for all six of the words are fixed on little stems and placed on the hot plate.

Paul is making coronet blossoms. Benchwork is critical to him as an artist. He creates every new element in his vocabulary, and masters it. Flower blossoms are Paul's passion, and his specialty. Figuring out how to make different varieties, how to translate each flower's particular intricacies into the unforgiving medium of glass, has been at the core of his art for years.

The coronet is not a flower you'll find in the fields. Five-petaled, of a pale lemon yellow, its crown of slender stamens giving it its name, it certainly has organic credibility. Paul recounts people poring through wild flower books to find it, and then calling him in desperation to find out what it was. The truth is, he made it up himself, inspired by his discovery that he could make long stamens and have them survive encapsulation in molten crystal. He was working on a real wild flower, the bright blue Asiatic day flower, an asymmetrical blossom with long curved stamens. When he experimented with encasing the stamens and found, to his amazement, that they didn't simply melt away or collapse as the 2000-degree crystal flowed around them, he dreamed up a new flower with long stamens. Thus the coronet was born. It is not the only flower Paul has created. The St. Anthony's flower is another he made up, the result of trying to produce a poppy in the studio.

To make the coronet, he begins with a "dot" of yellow glass, to which he affixes the crown of slender yellow stamens, each tipped with a button of amber. The stamens are each made by drawing out glass under the flame until it reaches the right thinness. Stamens in place, Paul then attaches each of the wedge-shaped petals he made previously this morning, lining them up slightly differently on each blossom to show the natural variation. He tends to case the yellow glass with white for these petals, because the white glass gives the petal a translucency that mimics the quality of actual flower petals. His goal is to make the flowers, even the created flowers, look real. (He recalls a moment of particular triumph when a newspaper art critic described his work as encasing live flowers in molten crystal.) The blossom complete, it joins its fellows on the hot plate.

There is a general discussion about what if any other flowers should be included in today's paperweight. Ultimately, it is decided to let the coronets stand on their own. Paul's decisions drive the work, but he is always open to input from Chris and Dave. Once members of the team are assigned their particular elements, it is they who then develop those elements further. "Christine makes honeybees better than I can," says Paul, "and she really developed the damselfly, with me looking over her shoulder." For now, Paul works on a segment of honeycomb, symbol of pollination. Having developed the honeycomb from hexagonal colorless canes cased in a milky white to imitate the beeswax, Paul assembles short slices of these canes onto a black ground, and then fuses them together in an oven. Fusing is a relatively recent addition to the technical repertoire of the studio, and in this case it allows for the creation of an endless variety of honeycomb configurations from the same basic elements.

Chris has turned her focus to a honeybee. Ocher glass is toned with casing of other shades of yellow or brown. Stripes of dark brown create the effect of black on the abdomen, the first part to be made. The thorax, and the head with its bulbous eyes, are

BUILDING A BEE *The thorax and abdomen, composed of black glass with light brown stripes, are sealed together in the flame. Next the head is sealed in place, and the wings are applied one by one and shaped with a hot colorless glass rod. Excess glass is drawn off to make the wings thin enough. The six fragile legs, of black glass filaments cased in colorless crystal, are braced together to stabilize them. The completed bee is sealed to a honeycomb cluster and the assemblage is flame-annealed to insure that the two parts are stable and will not crack.*

made in turn. Throughout the flameworking process, Chris is constantly melting and drawing the tips of the thin rods of glass with which she works. She likens it to "sharpening your pencil" to keep the working end of the glass rods the right size, allowing the benchworkers the precision they require. Six glass legs are attached to the thorax and will create a lifelike illusion when encased in crystal. The wings of the bee are the last element to be put in place. Pale amber glass, on hand from earlier preparation, is laced with thin threads of black, and then is tooled and flattened to form an accurate—organically credible—wing shape. She asks Paul if he wants the wings extended or folded back. Extended is the decision. The bee adds to the population on the hot plate.

Dave's final product is a "root person," one of the tawny little nude human figures Paul developed in the early 1980s. Recalling most vividly the lampwork figures of eighteenth-century Nevers, France, these earth spirits, both male and female, were created to inhabit the root systems of Paul's botanical sculptures, physical representations of the spirituality with which his work is infused. Today there is a lone female figure, recumbent, arms outstretched, to join the blossoms and blueberries on the hot plate.

During a lull in the conversation, Paul remarks on the repetitiveness of the benchwork. Again the image of a monastic scriptorium and manuscript illuminators jumps to mind. When working at the bench, a highly skilled flameworker can let his mind drift, just the way a skilled driver can cover long distances on an uncrowded highway without seeming to focus sharply on the act of driving. The mind, its pathways to the fingertips well worn and tried, works almost on automatic pilot, saving its reserves of sharpest concentration for the later, more intense parts of the process. Thus Paul, Christine, and David can listen to music and talk, to me and to each other, while at the bench, and even answer the telephone without breaking stride.

The glass door from the house slides open, and Patricia Stankard enters with a wave of cold air, armed with paychecks for David and Christine. Sebastian Kressley, at ten months, needs feeding. Flame jets are turned off, ovens are turned off, and the studio is shut down for lunch.

Learning to Love Glass Salem County Vocational Technical Institute had an open-door policy. Paul didn't need good grades to get in, only a willingness to try, and that, of course, was never the problem. Despite his marginal status as a student—because of

the as-yet undiscovered dyslexia—Paul was admitted. Right from the beginning he loved working with glass. "I saw the flames, and this activity, and I thought wow! This looks exciting." He was instantly seduced by the lure of the open flame and the opportunity to make things with his hands.

Half of each school day was spent learning how to blow glass. The other half of the day was taken up with technical courses to complement the manual skills he was developing. For the first time in his life there was a concrete payoff for studying hard, because the science courses made it easier for him to understand what he was doing and made the glassblowing itself easier. Before this, the concept of such benefits from study had eluded him, but now he began to apply himself. This was not glassblowing as art; far from it. This was highly skilled glassblowing geared toward the production of precision instruments for the chemical industry. The connection in Paul's mind between his newfound craft and the wild flowers that filled his free time was a long way off.

Enthusiasm didn't make up for Paul's learning disability, and he nearly failed his first year at Salem. His inability to cope adequately with the large amount of required technical reading and mathematics hampered his ability to learn glassblowing. At the end of his first year, the dean of the institute tried to persuade him to look elsewhere for a career. Paul's startling response was to simply refuse to leave. "No," he said, "I want to be a glassblower. I want to make glass instruments. I want to stay here." They let him stay. He got a summer job as a glassblower, and Salem put him on probation for his second year.

His summer job, like an old-fashioned apprenticeship, greatly increased his glassblowing skills. It was repetitive work, but it went a long way in helping Paul to master his craft. He worked in a factory, eight hours a day, and after nearly failing glassblowing his first year at Salem, he came back the second fall a far more skilled artisan. His first probationary semester ended with a B in glassblowing. He was also taking algebra both day and night in addition to his other course work. At night he was making up for flunking Algebra I his first year, and during the day Algebra II kept his mental gears spinning. He managed to pass both algebra courses and thus successfully completed the two-year program at Salem. His academic experience behind him, Paul did what he had always planned to do: he went into industry.

The first factory where Paul worked made laboratory apparatus for the petrochemical industry. A good deal of it was vessels and small-scale work, such as condensers, valves, stopcocks, and sealing joints on flasks. The appeal of glassblowing was its twofold demand, physical and mental. Paul loved being mentally engaged in the physical production of something. It wasn't abstract, or just figures on paper; his labor produced something concrete that he could see. He had managed to find a niche in American industry where the worker was still not disconnected from the product of his labor, and thus had found a place where he was, at long last, comfortable.

When he went home at night, Paul found himself thinking about his job, trying to figure out how to do it better. He found himself looking for challenges, ways to get better and more difficult jobs from his foreman at the factory. His motivation was a fear that he'd get "plugged in" at one skill level, once his skill was recognized. He didn't want to get stuck in one place and have to coast for the rest of his career doing one thing. Factory work was, if not actually tedious, certainly repetitive. His manual skills grew tremendously, and he continued to develop himself by moving around, both within one factory and from job to job. He was always eager to learn more about production techniques to add to his range of skills. Art had still not entered into the picture.

Paul's first job was for McAllister Scientific in Nashua, New Hampshire. After six months, homesick for New Jersey (and for his fiancée, Patricia Ann LaPatrick), he moved to Fisher Scientific in New York City. He loved that job and stayed there about a year. It was during this year that he married Patricia. A southern New Jersey native, Pat became Paul's partner as well as his spouse, and would play a critical role in Paul's career as an artist. In 1964 she left her job as a secretary at Campbell Soup in Camden and set about making a home for them, and for the five children who arrived as the years passed. Not wanting to uproot Pat and bring her to New York, he returned to the South Jersey glass industry, working at Andrews Glass Company in Vineland, where he earned $120 per week (with overtime) for about one year. Then came a short stint in the Virginia glass industry, followed by a four-year position with the Philco-Ford optical glass division in Spring City, Pennsylvania.

Throughout this eight-year period, 1963–71, Paul found that he was happy working with glass, but less and less content working in industry. For the very first time, while working at Andrews, he began to experiment in his free time with making lampwork animals—"knickknacks," both as a way to satisfy his creative urges and to supplement his income. Borrowing equipment to work with at first, he found that he loved creating things, and began to focus on it more seriously. For three years, between 1965 and 1967, he produced glass novelties and animals.

Around 1963 Paul befriended a longtime paperweight maker, Francis (Frank) Whittemore, whose work fascinated him. South Jersey had its own celebrated paperweight tradition, as well as a centuries-old tradition of glassblowers making ornamental objects after hours in their free time. Paul found himself yearning to make a paperweight, something that seemed far removed from anything he'd ever attempted. He began to experiment with paperweights, and by the fall of 1969 he'd given up glass animals entirely.

"I'd had it with production knickknacks. It was like working a full-time job at night to earn extra money with the glass animals. I wanted to do something more exciting, more significant." So in 1969, still with his day job in the chemical glass industry, Paul stopped everything else and began to focus exclusively on making paperweights.

Life, like a dome of many-coloured glass,
Stains the white radiance of Eternity,
Until Death tramples it to fragments.

PERCY BYSSHE SHELLEY, 1792–1822
Adonais (1821), LII

Making a Portrait of Nature

The pieces of the paperweight—leaves, blossoms, roots, the little word *murini*, the bee, and all the blueberries—are warm and stable on the hot plate when we return from lunch. Now comes the critical juncture in Paul's work. This is not the technical crisis (that will come later), but the artistic crisis. Paul Stankard doesn't just throw a few cute bits of glass together. He makes what he sees as his personal portraits of Nature; his personal vision of God's creative presence. Although he is proud of giving his elements "organic credibility," this is not, ultimately, what drives him.

"People who think that we've lost Nature have never walked down a highway and studied the wild flowers," he says. All morning long, as Paul and his staff have been working at the bench, melting and shaping bits of colored glass over the intense heat of the flame, Paul has been thinking about how he will arrange this paperweight, the one whose creation I have been invited to witness. Like a painter, Paul has spent the morning preparing his paints and his canvas, and laying out his brushes. Now comes the hard part.

While the many techniques involved in making paperweights have their roots in antiquity, the paperweight itself seems to be an exclusively Victorian phenomenon. Both French and Italian paperweights appeared on the market in 1845, although according to Robert Charleston, evidence suggests that there must have been some previous development. The French dominated the paperweight marketplace from the very beginning, due in large part to their use of a brilliantly clear dome of solid crystal to magnify the decorative components of the weight. The three major French houses, Clichy, Baccarat, and Saint-Louis, initially produced weights (the French term being *presse-papier*) using the Italian *millefiori* (thousand-flower) cane technique, dating back to ancient Roman glass. Canes were produced by arranging long strips of colored glass in patterns, then fusing them together. These canes were then drawn and sliced into the bright little floral motifs used in the early paperweights. By the middle of the nineteenth century, however, lampwork figures of fruit, flowers, and even animals had been added to the repertoire of the paperweight makers, both in Europe and in America. It is this sort of paperweight that first inspired Paul Stankard to abandon industry and look for the art in his glassmaking.

The major difference that separates Paul Stankard's work from that of the past and of his contemporaries is one of attitude, both spiritual and intellectual. Even the most ornate and glamorous of the Victorian French paperweights were nothing more than mass-produced inexpensive novelties, intended to lend a little sparkle to the desktops of well-appointed homes. The same had been true in the production of American paperweights—up until the moment when Paul Stankard began to look for something more than novelty and charm. Technical competence is not the end for Paul as it has been historically, but simply a means to something deeper.

A new flower in Paul's botanical vocabulary, or the addition of an insect, or the word canes, invariably represents a technical breakthrough, something new that can be achieved with hot glass. But each of these new elements is the result of an intellectual process, the search for meaning. This is not the conventionalized, sentimental "language of flowers" promulgated by the Victorians; this is the iconographic language of a sculptor. Technical prowess is simply the only way he can succeed.

As he begins to assemble the elements into the sculpture for the paperweight, Paul notes that each of the elements is like the most sophisticated, finely made instruments produced in glass for industry. The technical precision he learned in the factory has remained with him, and has made much of what he does possible.

He envisions the finished paperweight in three dimensions, in its several layers, physical and metaphysical. The honeycomb represents pollination, the beginning of the life cycle for all living things. The honeybee not only starts the cycle for flowering plants but has its own life cycle, which revolves around the honeycomb. Here the larval bees begin life, sheltered in the walls of their wax nurseries, fed with the honey produced from the nectar of the flowers.

The coronet blossoms go into place, representing the other side of pollination, the miraculous, delicate beauty that draws the bee and assures it of the sustenance it needs. The flower is essential for the life of the plant, and for the life of the bee. The blueberries represent fruition, but also the beginning of the end. The fruit provides sustenance for other creatures, from insects to humans; it is a necessary part of all creatures' life cycles. Yet the berry also represents the death of the flower. Paul's iconography rarely deals directly with the end of the life cycle; the fruit itself only alludes to the coming withering and decay, when winter brings the temporary death that ends with the return of spring—the renewal of the eternal cycle. There is also a seasonal aspect in his work, as Paul points out. Often, what you see in his crystalline capsules reflects what he sees out his windows.

Beneath this layer will be another layer, visible only when the paperweight is turned over. Long ago Paul abandoned the "one-sided" paperweight. His work is full of small surprises. Below the honeycomb and the berries will be the roots, and the word canes, and the recumbent female form of the earth spirit. The root people are reminders both of humanity and of Divine presence. Their intention is to make the visible connection that the life of the wild flower is closely akin to that of the human. For Paul, the wild flower is a microcosm of human life. Despite our arrogance and apparent physical powers, Paul seems to suggest that we are not greater than the wild flower: We are the result of Creation, no more and no less than any other living thing, equally subject to the laws of Nature. Above the sculpture, hovering in its own crystalline sky, will be the honeybee, mediator between the animal and vegetable worlds.

Even if all the technical hurdles are successfully leapt, not every paperweight that comes from the annealing oven leaves the studio. Nor does every painting from an artist's easel work in the end, nor every sculpture in an atelier come out right. Sometimes that cannot be known until the very end. "I may not be the smartest guy in the world," says Paul, "but I'm smart enough to know how to protect the integrity of my work. You'll never see a failed Stankard on the market." Around the studio sit various not-quite-completed paperweights and botanicals. These are not spoiled by flaws or technical problems. These are works that just don't seem "right." Sometimes they sit for months or even years, until Paul can achieve enough distance to see what's good about them. Sometimes they are slipped quietly into a drawer, never to see the light of day.

"The work is most satisfying to me when the spiritual quality comes through," says Paul. Mere prettiness, and even technical perfection, sometimes are just not enough.

Becoming an Artist When Paul decided to dedicate himself to making paperweights, there was nothing written about the technical side of it. Historically, paperweight making, like so many aspects of the glassblower's trade, was shrouded in a sort of alchemist's secrecy. So Paul took what he already knew about the properties of hot glass and blundered headlong into his dream. Between 1969 and 1971 he experimented with paperweights, making what he looks back on as stupid mistakes (sometimes repeatedly), and gradually teaching himself the new technical skills he needed to know. Reinventing the wheel, so to speak, was a difficult task, but Paul kept at it simply because he was in love with the idea of making beautiful things. He still had his day job, and the concept of becoming an artist had not yet occurred to him. All he was doing was seeking some way to do more with his God-given talents than make anonymous bits of precision equipment for industry.

It wasn't until 1971 that Paul first showed a few of his creations to some antique dealers who carried old paperweights, and to some of the dealers who specialized in the paperweight market. As anyone who has worked in the decorative arts field can tell you, there is a specialized collecting market for nearly every aspect of the decorative arts, no matter how obscure or narrowly focused it may seem. The market for antique French paperweights was (and remains) intensely competitive. Paul was gratified that his early pieces were accepted and acknowledged to be "pretty nice." His first weights sold for twenty dollars.

Looking back, Paul recalls that these first paperweights were good, but that they did not have the technical or aesthetic quality of pieces by the masters of the day, Charles Kaziun and Francis Whittemore. At twenty-eight, Paul was showing early promise, but he was still a long way from doing what he wanted to do technically. He certainly had not begun to approach his work from the point of view of creativity. "It took me five years of paperweight making to become creative," he notes. Coming from a technical background, with no foundation in art history or aesthetics, Paul had no personal vocabulary for artistic concepts. "I just wanted to make beautiful paperweights, and to do them well." It was at this point he turned to the inspiration of his childhood, to the solace of his schooltime struggles, the wild flowers that grew all around him in the South Jersey sunshine. No one guided him in this direction. As he puts it: "That's where my bliss led me."

Paul hadn't a clue how to make the flowers, didn't know how to produce the antique floral weights he so admired. His first efforts were attempts to interpret the wild flowers in his mind's eye. He had no idea whether or not there was any market for his vision. The first response to his work was positive, and, needless to say, it made him feel great. Paul began to study antique French weights, and to talk to paperweight dealers. As modest as the prices were for his weights, it was far more than the thirty-five cents he'd been able to fetch for one of his little glass animals. People liked what he was doing, and were willing to pay him twenty dollars for it. It was a rush, and it inspired him to new efforts to expand both his skills and his aesthetic horizon.

In the summer of 1971 Paul taught his father-in-law, Walter LaPatrick, to make the little lampwork animals that he had long since abandoned. Having arranged for a booth at the Indian Summer Art Show in Atlantic City to sell his glass souvenirs, Paul's father-in-law offered to try to sell some of Paul's newest paperweights as well. While the weights were on display in Mr. LaPatrick's booth, Reese Palley, an Atlantic City gallery owner, happened by. He was immediately taken with Paul's work, and told LaPatrick that he wanted to give him a show in the gallery.

Palley specialized in the high priced, decorative porcelain flower-and-bird sculptures produced by the Edward Marshall Boehm Company, of Trenton, New Jersey. He obviously knew the market for beautiful, well-crafted objects. He gave Paul his first gallery show, and sold every one of the paperweights. Rare is the sold-out gallery exhibition for even well-established artists today. For an untried artist like Paul, it was nothing short of a revelation.

Palley clearly felt he was onto something, and urged Paul to make as many paperweights as he could, convinced he could sell everything Paul sent him. Paul demurred. Pat was expecting their fourth child, and Paul, by this time working for Rohm & Haas, was still only making paperweights in his spare time. Palley, undeterred, told Paul that he should be working full-time at his craft, and even promised to make sure that Paul could support his family and make money with his paperweights. Paul went to Pat and laid his cards on the table. He wanted this chance to work on his paperweights full-time. Pat struck a simple deal with her husband. Paul had to wait until two weeks after the baby was born. Thus, two weeks after Joseph Paul Stankard entered this world, Paul Joseph Stankard left forever the world of industry.

Of the first batch of ten paperweights that Paul brought to Reese Palley's gallery, six were rejected as not good enough. If Palley was going to be Paul's meal ticket, he wasn't going to settle for second-best. After that, determined to succeed, Paul did better. Early on, he produced ten to fifteen paperweights a week for Palley, and Palley never again rejected any of them. That initial rejection had been an important lesson in quality, and one that Paul never forgot. Like it or not, Paul had become an artist, and could now dedicate himself, and the future of his family, to his art. Patricia now took on her second major role in Paul's life, one she plays to this day, that of his business manager. From this point on, Pat was immersed in the daily routine of running Paul's studio, a job that has grown with Paul's success. From the start Pat supported Paul's vision, and her capable handling of the business aspects of his career enabled him to pursue his dream.

Confident of her parenting skills, Patricia was willing to do without so that Paul could buy the tools he needed to make paperweights. His first year on his own, Paul cleared $6,000. He'd been making $10,500 in 1972 at Rohm & Haas, a good salary for the time. So they sold one of their two cars, and Pat mended the kids' clothes and made a lot of sandwiches to stretch their food budget, but at least he was making money. The second year out Paul made $7,200—a twenty percent increase. And every year thereafter it got better. It had been a long shot, but it paid off. Eventually finances became strong enough to allow him to hire his first assistant, John Glass, in 1975, to help in the benchwork preparation of the numerous elements for the individual pieces. This freed Paul to spend more time thinking creatively, to improve his work. This was also the year Paul bought a special order of 5,000 pounds of soda-lime crystal from Schott Optical Glass.

This quantity of glass, which would make his paperweights sparkle, cost him $15,000, for which he had to remortgage his house. Again the gamble paid off.

Throughout the 1970s, Paul's reputation grew, and he began to become well known for his floral paperweights. Indeed, Paul's early paperweights look rather like some of the French floral weights of the mid-nineteenth century: simple, colorful, stylized flowers of no readily recognizable botanical variety, sometimes set against a colored ground. His craftsmanship was apparent, and his work gained instant respect, from collectors and other glass artists as well.

By the mid-1970s, the Smithsonian Institution, having included Paul's work in an exhibition on contemporary glass and ceramics, expressed interest in having some of Paul's paperweights for its permanent collection. Paul went to his father, then struggling with terminal illness, and proposed that he might donate some paperweights to the Smithsonian. For the elder Stankard, it was a source of great pride that his son, who had been foolhardy enough to leave a stable job to pursue a life of art, was not only supporting his family, but was good enough to be wanted by the nation's largest museum. Two Stankard weights were donated in the name of Martin Francis Stankard before his death in 1976. In 1977 Paul began a limited-edition series of paperweights for the Smithsonian, and in 1982 another series for the Art Institute of Chicago.

It was Paul's sense of artistic mission that appears to have first set him apart from the quasi-folk-art world of the old-time paperweight craftsmen like Kaziun and Whittemore. His desire to develop and expand his art brought him to the notice of the early leaders of the studio glass movement, glassblowers with a training in studio art. It was at this point that Paul first began to find himself in the company of men like Dominick Labino and Harvey Littleton, men who had been grappling with glass as an artistic medium since the 1950s.

In 1975 Paul attended a seminar on paperweights in Wisconsin. There he met and talked with many of the important names of the day, when studio glass was still a fledgling movement. He was exhilarated and confident in his work, but he realized in talking to these people that he was seen as being somehow on the periphery of contemporary glass, outside the mainstream. He could see that the glass artists were having more fun than he was. They were expressing themselves more fully in their work, stretching the material to meet their artistic needs. It was a very different tradition than the one from which Paul came, and he envied their originality. Paul wanted somehow to be a part of this larger category of "glass art." Once again, as he had when he discovered paperweights, he became hungry to learn.

Paul's goal for the latter half of the 1970s was to broaden his horizons, to learn how to take the paperweight tradition and run with it. He began to see his early success with floral paperweights as only the beginning, a starting point. He began to listen to classical music seriously for the first time, marveling at its longevity and the mystery of its unfading allure. The baroque lushness of Bach and Vivaldi got him hooked, and he expanded to the sparkling classicism of Mozart and the stormy romanticism of Beethoven. He began to collect books, although his newly understood dyslexia continued to hamper his efforts at reading. He listened to the radio, to educational programs, absorbing everything he could that would give him more breadth, a greater frame of reference. A bolt from the blue struck him from the radio, from a program on WHYY, a classical station out of Philadelphia. Two commentators were discussing excellence, and one of them stated that in order to do excellent work, you had to be able to recognize excellence, and not just in your own field, but in art, in literature, and in music. Artistic achievement was a constant quest for excellence. A simple enough concept, but it hit Paul like an electric charge, and made him determined to take risks, to be original, to truly become the artist he wanted to be. Paul had a new goal: to contribute to the history of glass, not just at the periphery, but at its center.

> *What could it be like to labor day after day to produce an object of great beauty, a legacy of spirituality as well as aesthetic triumph?*
>
> SUSAN HOWATCH, 1940–
> *The Rich Are Different* (1977)

Capturing Nature If the creation of the individual elements for a paperweight is the most important part of a day's work, the encapsulation of the flamework sculpture is the most mentally and physically intense. This is where disasters happen. There are a number of points of no return in this process. But this is also where, in some ways, the true magic takes place.

Chris places a biscuit-shaped piece of commercial colorless crystal, called a gob, on a small rotating platform, where it is given its initial heating under flame. The top part of the sculptural "bouquet" is placed on a circular iron plate and set inside a small electric oven, about the size of a bread box and shaped like a Quonset hut. Chris transfers the crystal gob to a blowing rod, or pontil, and then, after the top is "peeled" to remove any possible imperfections or dirt, hands it to Dave to place in the glory hole of a small, drum-shaped, gas-fired furnace, heated to 2000 degrees Fahrenheit. A second crystal gob is placed on the rotating platform. All of this is performed with a carefully choreographed casualness that belies the care and precision needed to do it right. The heat in the studio is mounting steadily, to the point that the ninety-degree breeze outside feels cool in the door-way where I position myself to be out of the way.

A cast-iron collar is placed on the plate with the lampworked flowers. When the par-tial sculpture has been heated to a compatible temperature, Paul guides the red-hot gob of crystal from the glory hole and Dave opens the oven. Aided by a vacuum pump (to draw off the air) and an air spray nozzle, Paul places the molten crystal gob on top of the frag-ile glass flowers. He and Dave call me over to look closely, and the intense heat blasts upward as I bend down to see. The delicate little stamens of the coronet blossoms are standing proud, glowing red-hot in their new fiery mantle. A Sunday-school image of the flames of Hell crosses my mind, as the elements of the sculpture glow red, then seem to turn brown as in death. The first successful part of the paperweight is taken aside to fire-polish, still on the pontil.

Meanwhile the second, lower layer of the sculpture is placed on the iron plate in the oven, and the collar set in place. The second gob of crystal is peeled and placed on the pontil in the glory hole. A third, smaller gob of crystal is set rotating before the flame. When the temperature is right, the second half of the paperweight is made the same way as the first. The little earth spirit's delicate limbs have survived the heat, the word canes are in position in the roots of the plants. This second half of the weight, on its pontil, is fire-polished, while the honeybee is placed on the iron plate in the oven. Then both halves of the paperweight are reheated to bring them to compatible temperatures, and Paul, holding one pontil in each hand, presses the red-hot halves together. He comments, as he eyeballs the positioning of the two parts ("lining up the blueberries"), that there is some latitude for creativity at this moment, because you can decide just how you want to line things up. The first pontil is broken off, and the top of the paperweight is fire-polished

1

2

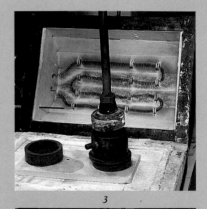

3

4

5

6

7

8

9

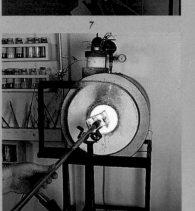

10

11

12

13

14

15

16

17

18

19

20

MAKING A BOTANICAL *(1) The completed parts of the botanical sculpture, including flowers, roots, and earth spirit figures, are kept on a hot plate until the final construction process begins. (2) The sections of the botanical are produced in the same way a paperweight is made: part of the sculpture is placed in a circular iron collar and heated in the oven. (3) Colorless molten crystal, on a pontil rod, is then placed on top of the sculpture in the collar. (4) This process is repeated for the next section, after which the two sections are joined together. (5) The half-finished botanical is then placed in the carbon block mold to give it the proper shape. (6, 7, & 8) Each succeeding part of the botanical—which can be the equivalent of three complete paperweights in terms of material and work time—is "stacked" on its predecessor, and all sections must be kept hot to avoid the danger of cracking and destroying the entire piece. (9, 10, & 11) A completed botanical is placed once more in the carbon block mold for shaping, then inspected for surface impurities and cleaned at the flame. (12) At this point it can be placed in the computer-controlled annealing oven for the slow, gradual process of cooling. The final steps include cutting and polishing the botanical's surfaces. (13, 14) If it is to be a cloistered botanical, the piece is sent to Jim Shaw, in Oregon, who laminates the plates of dark colored glass to the polished surfaces. (15, 16, & 17) Once the colored glass has adhered, the final cutting and polishing can be completed on the cloistered botanical (18, 19, & 20).*

once more. Paul sets the pontil on a stand with rollers, and applies a carbon blocking tool to the red-hot crystal, to round and shape it into the characteristic domed form.

Paul, at this point soaked through with sweat, asks, "Dave, where's the bee?" Dave pauses, then says, "West—Jimmy's house." Paul responds, "Flying to Jimmy's." Chris just smiles at my confusion, until it dawns on me that Paul is visualizing the orientation of the glass honeybee, on its back in the oven. Paul tells Dave to push the bee a little off center, then brings the reheated, nearly complete paperweight over. The bee is pressed into the top of the paperweight, and the last of the three red-hot crystal gobs is placed over it and trimmed. Paul gets the spherical cane segment with his initials and the year in it and inserts it neatly into the side of the completed paperweight, melting off the outer face to smooth it into the side. Then he returns to the bench, and begins to shape and smooth the paperweight with the carbon blocking tool. Dave and Chris start to shut down the furnace and the oven.

As he works with the blocking tool, the technical crisis past, Paul tells me that, for one of the botanicals, the block-shaped paperweights he developed in the early 1980s, it will take at least five gobs, or pick-ups, of crystal to totally encase the sculpture. Dave shows me the hinged carbon mold in which the botanicals are shaped. Then, just as we're winding down, Paul says, "Uh oh, Chris, your bee separated." We go over and look, and sure enough, the abdomen has "floated" away from the rest of it, leaving a bisected bee hovering over the coronets and blueberries. "This sort of thing happens," Paul remarks philosophically. "The insects are so fragile, and the heat is intense. We'll just have to peel it off."

The glory hole is fired up again, another little gob of crystal is set to heating, and Paul rotates the dome of the paperweight in the flame until he can peel the hapless honeybee away. "So," he says, "we'll have a paperweight without a bee." He shapes the paperweight with the blocking tool, fire-polishing it at the flame. This process takes some time, and Dave and Chris complete the shutdown of the other equipment. Paul shows me the finished weight, the flamework sculpture still glowing inside its crystal sphere. I can't really see it clearly, for it is distorted by the heat. Then it goes into an electric annealing oven controlled by computer. Starting at 968 degrees Fahrenheit, the temperature will gradually drop over the next fifteen hours, regulated by the computer, to prevent cracking. A botanical block will take thirty hours to anneal. "Before I had this computer," Paul says, "I was a very busy boy." And if the power goes out? A whole day's work is shattered.

Expanding the Vision From the beginning of his success, Paul had to battle the two basic prejudices against his work in the Studio Glass Movement: content and scale. The fact that he worked in a small-scale, representational tradition, and with flowers as his primary subject, seemed to place him in some glass netherworld of church bazaars and airport gift shops—at least in some people's eyes. The paperweight collectors were devoted to him from the start, but this wing of the glass world had always been, and remains today, something of a subculture. In the 1970s and 80s the art world was grappling with abstraction, minimalism, and large-scale gestures, and every part of the craft-as-art world was infected with the desire to be "big" and "powerful." By the early 80s, craft artists were turning their backs defiantly on the roots of their craft, seeking some indefinable status as "pure" artists. Of all the craft media, studio glass artists were perhaps the most deeply influenced by this yearning for artistic status. For an artist like Paul, coming from the centuries-old lampwork tradition, and for whom the representation of nature was the spiritual core of his work, this attitude posed a real dilemma.

In 1979, The Corning Museum of Glass in Corning, New York, possibly the greatest collection of glass in the world, mounted a survey exhibition of contemporary glass. The exhibition and its companion publication traveled throughout the United States. Paul submitted ten slides to the jurying for the exhibition and was rejected. Already acknowledged as one of the leaders among paperweight makers worldwide, he was frustrated at this exclusion. The following year, however, he was invited to Corning to give a lecture at the Corning Glass Seminar. Corning has a celebrated collection of paperweights, and this year the focus of the seminar was on this part of their vast collection. Paul, who is articulate and captivating when he talks about his work, spoke to an audience of three hundred people, and received a standing ovation. William Warmus, then a curator at Corning, came up to Paul afterward and congratulated him, praising his work highly. When Paul wryly commented that he'd been rejected from the New Glass Review, Warmus's comment to him was that the exclusion had been a mistake. Such was the position in which Paul found himself in 1980 vis-à-vis the Studio Glass Movement: wild approbation from those who could see past the small scale and traditional content of his work, and respectful, but arms-length curiosity from those who were bound by the dogmas of modern art.

Another watershed came in November 1979, when Paul went to an exhibition at the

Franklin Institute in Philadelphia called "The Courage to Create." This was during his period of hungry learning. The Franklin's show highlighted the work of thirteen widely-ranging creative visionaries, analyzing and dissecting their work, from Buckminster Fuller to Judy Chicago, from John Cage to Jasper Johns. It was an astonishing assemblage of creative talent, and Paul found himself completely baffled. He couldn't figure out the common thread, other than the fact that each person had made a name for themselves in their field. He went back to the show a second time, with his brother, still puzzled by what he saw. His brother clarified things for him. What linked these people together was their willingness to take risks, to experiment. These were all people who took chances, who looked for new ways to do things. It was another epiphany for Paul. He returned to his Mantua studio and didn't make another paperweight for months. He began, instead, to experiment.

Out of these experiments in the early months of 1980 came the form for which Paul is most celebrated, the botanical. Early attempts produced vaguely rectangular blocks, looking rather like melting ice, encasing a floral sculpture that could be viewed not just from the top, as in a paperweight, but from all sides. Even though paperweights are three-dimensional objects, they are conceived as being seen from one direction—above. What Paul had produced was something that had to be studied in the round, including from beneath. No one had ever thought of looking at the bottom of a paperweight. Here was another revelation. The creation of the botanical didn't turn him away from the traditional paperweight form, but, aside from literally doubling his formal repertoire, it offered him a new way to think about the paperweight form. There was no reason one couldn't make paperweights that were as three-dimensional in conception as the botanical format, paperweights that didn't just sit there, but that required close-up examination and needed to be turned this way and that to be fully appreciated. So the botanical was not only an entirely new horizon in itself, but it infused new life into the paperweight tradition.

Around the time Paul first developed the botanical format, he was producing between two hundred and two hundred fifty paperweights each year. He drove himself fairly hard, knowing that his income depended on sales, and sales depended on successfully completed paperweights. The popularity of the paperweights supported his experimental work on the botanical series. For a while, he even devoted every Friday and Saturday exclusively to producing a single botanical. Every technical challenge was a chance to learn, and every hurdle safely leapt was a new addition to his artistic vocabulary.

Around this time Paul had lost interest in merely imitating the antique French paper-weights. Even the masters of the day, Kaziun and Whittemore, were more or less still root-ed in the French traditions. Their flowers, expertly crafted, were stylized, whimsical, decorative. Paul wanted to produce work that was unique, that looked as personal as it felt to him. This began a renewed study of wild flowers, something no one else in his tra-dition was dealing with, and something that had rich associations for Paul. Paul began to look at wild flowers, not as something to be abstracted to suit the medium of glass, but as something that he needed to translate into a new language. Not having been to art school, and thus not having been trained to care about "art issues" that seemed to obsess his peers in the studio glass world, Paul looked for his own issues. What rose to the fore was the religious feeling inculcated in him by his Irish Catholic upbringing in New En-gland. This merged with his intense love of Nature and concern for the environment. All around him, as suburban sprawl began to eat up South Jersey farmland, and New Jersey itself developed a national notoriety for pollution, Paul saw the radical disjunction between humanity and Nature. Once more, a simple enough concept, but one with the potential to infuse a greater power into his work. Wild flowers were the physical expression of God's word, and Paul wanted to transcribe that word in glass. He wanted people to be able to see the wondrousness of creation in his paperweights.

A central figure in the development of Paul's vision of nature was Michael Diorio. Diorio had first come of know of Paul's work through Reese Palley's gallery in Atlantic City. A dentist by profession, he was a nature photographer by avocation, and Palley sug-gested to him that he should get in touch with Stankard. With their shared enthusiasm for wild flowers, Paul and Michael quickly became close friends. They would travel around the pine barrens together, Diorio photographing the wild flowers that Paul would exper-iment with in his flameworking. In frequent telephone conversations they would com-pare notes and share information about their mutual fascination with wild flowers. Paul became a fan of Michael's photography, and Diorio became an avid collector of Stankard paperweights.

A new threshold had been crossed, and Paul's celebrity grew. His work was enthu-siastically embraced by collectors in Europe as well as in the United States. The startling difference of his paperweights from anything that had preceded them made them popu-lar with collectors of antique paperweights as well as collectors of modern weights. His work was now fetching from one thousand to twenty-five hundred dollars. Collecting "Stankards" became its own category in paperweight circles, and serious collectors would own upwards of fifty examples of his work. A secondary marketplace—at auction—appeared. This is always a test for contemporary art, and something with little precedent in the craft media. Early paperweights that Paul had sold for a couple hundred dollars were being knocked down for two thousand.

By this time Paul had his own dealers, a primary one being Leo Kaplan, on Madison Avenue in New York City. His work was also represented by L. H. Selman, Ltd., in Santa Cruz, California. Douglas Heller, of Soho's Heller Gallery, gave Paul a one-man show in 1979. This was something of a crossover show for Paul, and it sold out, most likely due to Paul's large following. Collectors of Stankard paperweights did not generally frequent contemporary glass galleries. Heller was a new kind of venue for Stankard, and it placed him in the context of contemporary studio glass. As the best craftsman in his field, even if still at the periphery, Paul was being taken seriously. He was traveling and meeting other glass artists. He knew what was going on in contemporary studio glass, and knew that he was still on the margins; but he also knew that he was no longer being excluded. The quality of his work had forced the glass world to take note.

Paul found, however, that contemporary glass collectors didn't collect the way paperweight collectors did. They bought encyclopedically, that is, one piece by one artist, one piece by another. Rarely did they assemble groups of work by a single artist. So, while Paul found himself in collections full of names like Dale Chihuly, Harvey Littleton, Flora Mace, Joey Kirkpatrick, Mark Peiser, he found fewer repeat buyers. The difference was that paperweight enthusiasts collected Paul's work for its content, whereas studio glass aficionados bought it for its form. One paperweight, or one botanical, was seen as adequate for a broad glass collection. Studio glass artists were very much form-driven, as were most craft artists. A collector who owned a Dale Chihuly sea-form would wait until some drastic change happened in his work before acquiring another. Outwardly, Paul's work didn't change, and thus it seemed to be a dead-end to many collectors.

Paperweight buffs, on the other hand, looked for every subtle shift in Paul's work, every new addition to his vocabulary, every variation in the message of his increasingly complex iconography. Studio glass collectors didn't quite get the point, at least at first. Paul was puzzled, needless to say, and not a little disappointed. If people didn't read just one play by Shakespeare, or buy paintings based solely on their shape, then why would they feel that a single Stankard somehow said everything that needed to be said in their collection?

One pivotal collector in Paul's career was Mike Belkin. A collector of antique French paperweights, Belkin first saw Paul's work at an auction in New York City. He bought a few of Paul's paperweights and finally telephoned him, getting an immediate invitation to the studio. He and Paul became fast friends, sharing both a love of paperweights and a love of nature. Belkin built up a major collection of both Stankard paperweights and botanical sculptures, and also developed an interest in other contemporary studio glass through his knowledge of Paul's work. Belkin's fifty-two-acre property next to a nature reserve has become a favorite spot for Paul. Moreover, Mike has provided sage business management advice to Paul and Patricia over the past fifteen years. His support and friendship have helped Paul flourish and thrive as a studio artist.

By the end of the 1980s, Paul had some success in educating more of his growing audience to expand their understanding of his work. Thus, today, there are collectors of studio glass who collect his work in depth as it evolves.

The botanical format took years to develop, both artistically and economically. Gradually, the single botanical produced each week began to pay for itself in the marketplace, and Paul began a slow transition, by the end of the 1980s, to exclusive use of the rectangular block format. This was another gamble, because the form confused collectors, but Paul felt it was more important, artistically, than the paperweight format had been. In the blocklike shape of the botanical, the delicate glass flowers truly became sculptural, and each piece could be more challenging, technically and intellectually, than the last.

As the botanical format began to displace the paperweight, Paul began to explore other ways to add new elements to his work. The most radical of these was the inclusion of earth spirits, what he called his root people. His constant quest for new knowledge and self-education had led him to search for some way to express the metaphysical interconnection between humankind and Nature. He was moved by the concept of nature spirits that he learned of from Zen Buddhism and other Eastern philosophies, but couldn't identify with it emotionally. Too deeply grounded in Western religion, too bound to his own Judeo-Christian beliefs, he reinterpreted this notion of nature spirit. The result, inspired by anthropomorphic illustrations in medieval herbal books, was the elegant mottled human figures that began to appear more and more frequently in the root systems of his

botanical flower sculptures. They are mythical creatures, seemingly evocative of all creation theologies, but in fact more closely tied to the Eden of Judeo-Christian theology. Paul's root people are nothing more or less than a concrete visual reminder of mankind's inseparable connection with all life on earth, and of all life's inseparable connection to God.

"My work is my prayer," says Paul, expressing a spirituality that is ever present, but which he rarely verbalizes. A Latin motto on the ventilation hood over his workbench reads *Laborare est Orare,* to work is to pray. All of it, the earth spirits, the word canes, the insects, the flower blossoms themselves, are words, and his botanicals and paperweights are prayers rendered in glass.

> *The Devil whispered behind the leaves,*
> *"It's pretty, but is it Art?"*
>
> RUDYARD KIPLING, 1865–1936
> *The Conundrum of the Workshops*

Cloisters and Kilns Paul's work has been described by his most ardent fans, and to his bemusement, as miniature. Truthfully, many of the elements in his paperweights and botanicals are smaller than life, but that is incidental. Paul's work is small in scale; it is made the way it is meant to be seen, close up, intimately. Paul observes nature closely in order to create new visions in his work. The viewer, too, must observe closely, in order to understand what Paul is saying.

When the finished paperweight ends its fifteen-hour incarceration in the gradually decreasing heat of the annealing oven, it will still need finishing touches, including more polishing and Paul's engraved signature. Each of his pieces is assigned a permanent number, for Paul, with Christine and Patricia's help, keeps detailed records, both written and photographic.

Botanicals have a longer preparation time before they're ready for the marketplace, however. Some of this has to do with their inherent differences from paperweights; some of it has to do with Paul's ongoing struggle with issues of scale. Botanicals are molded in a hinged block, and when they come out of the annealing oven they need to be polished at a lapidary wheel, just as a large gemstone, or scientific optical glass, needs to be polished. Polishing defines the edges as sharply as Paul desires, and brings out the sparkling clarity of the crystal block. The fresh-from-the-oven botanical has its own appeal, the look of melted ice blurring the floral sculpture trapped inside. Sometimes Paul will have only some of the faces of the botanical polished smooth, leaving the sides textured. As a curator I am drawn to these, because the unpolished surfaces impart to the piece an unexpected tactile quality, something not associated with paperweights traditionally. Curators have a professional habit of wanting to handle things, and these textured botanicals are awfully inviting.

A major change in the late 1980s was the development of what Paul calls his "cloistered" botanicals. They are somewhat larger than his earliest botanicals, and he further alters and enlarges them by having plates of dark blue or green glass—transparent, but barely—laminated to the back and sometimes the sides as well. This enshrines—cloisters—the floral sculpture, forcing the viewer into a one-perspective approach. Unlike the early paperweights, this doesn't make the piece two-dimensional, but rather renders it like a statue in a niche. One sees it in three dimensions, but the viewer's access to the piece is controlled by the artist. Cloistering also makes the pieces more massive, among the largest works Paul has ever created. The studio glass world, the craft world, and the art world generally, have a deeply ingrained prejudice against smallness. Though fiercely proud of his smallest paperweights, Paul nonetheless seeks ways to expand his scale. Paul has even paired his botanical sculptures, cloistering them together to form still larger compositions called diptychs and triptychs. More recently still, working in collaboration with Winston-Salem–based glass artist Jon Kuhn, who specializes in laminating layers of glass, Paul has had one of his botanicals encased in a glittering mantle of laminated optical crystal. Nearly two feet tall, it is unquestionably a glamorous object, but what makes it work is the little botanical sculpture at its heart.

The cloistering process is not done in the studio, but by Jim Shaw, a professional glassworker who knows the technique. Glass technology is always state of the art in Paul's work, and he believes in exploiting technology to make his work better. Technologically, Paul's studio work is as up to date as any scientific factory setting. He shows me a cloistered botanical, but in this case a disaster—one that fractured side to side during the cloistering process. "Better to have it break at this point than once it gets into someone's home."

Paul has begun to experiment in his own studio, in the basement of the little green house-*cum*-gallery next door, with kiln casting as an alternative to laminated cloistering.

He shows me several unfinished botanicals, their sides and bottoms covered with plates of pale, sky blue crystal. These plates are fused to the body of the botanical, not glued up. This is something he would like to develop himself, to do in his own studio. Polished up, they should be beautiful, Paul assures me, although he wants to tinker with the color. Rows of slabs of melted colored glass cover a table in the experimental lab, waiting for further forays into the kiln. However, this is just the beginning. The path to be taken is not yet clear, and, Paul admits to me as we leave the studio for the day, he has no idea where he'll be in five years.

Riding the Crest

"Some days the most important thing in my life is promoting the beauty of the wild flower in my work. On other days, the most important thing is finishing by 2:30." Paul admits this with the clear-eyed pragmatism that has always lain behind his artistic vision. Paul Stankard is, at day's end, a humble man, fully aware of the fragility of his success. The only reason he has remained at the bench for twenty-three years, producing his intimate treasures in lampwork and crystal, is that it has been a good living for him. He has been a tremendous success, and being a success was, and still is, important to him. His botanicals today will fetch from six thousand to thirteen thousand dollars, depending on their size and complexity. A triptych's three botanicals cloistered together bring him twenty-two thousand dollars. As much as he loves his work, he would have abandoned it long ago had it not allowed him to support his wife and children. Or he might have adopted a more commercial approach to glass. He and Patricia have lived a completely traditional life, and Paul marvels at the miracle of it. Even though he has been accepted into "the gang" of contemporary glass artists, he knows that he is still in some ways outside their realm, both personally and artistically, because he has not had formal art training. He does not see himself as driven the way other glass artists are, but he is nonetheless something of a workaholic. He organizes his day around the rhythm of his family, because being a good father is important to him, but he keeps his studio time sacred. The three oldest children are out of college and on their own, his younger son is still in college, and his youngest child, Philip, now thirteen, is at home. Paul accommodates his schedule to be able to pick up Philip at school, play a game of baseball with him, or take him crabbing in the Delaware River. On the other hand, Paul's evenings and weekends are often filled with meetings, telephone calls, and preparations for upcoming exhibitions. Patricia and Christine are always right beside him, assisting in the essential business of being a success.

Life as an artist is not without its career frustrations, of course. Benchwork, critical as it is, can be grueling. When he started working full-time back in 1972, Paul found he could only sit at the bench for two hours at a stretch. He just didn't have enough energy to go longer. Now, somewhat to his surprise, he finds he can work with real concentration for eight or ten hours at a time if he needs to. His attention span has grown. He can give a week's energy to a single botanical work, and find that he still has more to give it.

Spontaneity, on the other hand, is not part of his work. Glass artists such as Dale Chihuly and Harvey Littleton thrive on spontaneity, make it part of their creative process. Paul cannot. His work evolves scientifically, due both to his training and to the nature of the craft itself. New things are arrived at by experimentation, trial and error. Paul feels that if he'd gone into a fine arts program rather than a technical one, he never would have taken the direction he took. Creativity is hampered by flameworking, and to some degree by glass itself. Paul became a precision craftsman first, and only then did he evolve into an artist. Freedom only comes with the mastering of a particular skill, the repeated successful creation of a difficult plant until it has been firmly rooted in his brain. For example, in 1990 he began to work on developing America's most beautiful native flowering shrub, the mountain laurel. With all its articulated petals, it was a real technical challenge. After weeks of experimentation, discarding flawed or failed efforts, he finally got it right. Now the mountain laurel is part of his botanical vocabulary. Eventually he may become bored with a particular blossom and set it aside.

Glass is unforgiving and limiting, almost inimical to the feelings Paul is trying to express. His medium fights him every inch of the way. The only spontaneous part of Paul's work is in the ideas, and that truth has led him in recent years to poetry. His poems are all in free verse, densely written, in a way that parallels the closely observed nature of his work. Also, his poems are largely about flowers and plants, and honeybees. Often his poetry coincides with the work he is producing in the studio, allowing his expression far more free rein than the flame does, letting him verbalize emotions that simply cannot be translated into glass. Paul says his poetry has allowed him to delve further into nature. There are no people in his poems, not even his root people. Like the work itself, Paul's poems are prayers. Most typically, the poems are printed out on the computer, and accompany

Forget-Me-Nots with Honeybees. 1991. Engraved: Paul J. Stankard A7; D. 3½". Belkin Collection

various paperweights and botanicals. Boxed in plastic frames, they line the central beam of his studio. The poems appear in exhibitions with his work, and have been published, both on their own and alongside his pieces. Now and then he has had a poem engraved on the back of a cloistered botanical where it won't interfere with the work itself, but allows another entry point for the viewer seeing the work.

Hand in hand with the poetry goes another recent acquisition, a parcel of woodland he purchased half a dozen years ago. A few miles from his house lie his six acres. They include sandy paths, ravines, rock formations, and even some frontage on a small river, surrounded by farmland and meadows. This untouched tract has become his visual laboratory, where he can walk, study nature, and seek inspiration for his work and his poetry. The core of his inspiration is in this sort of terrain, and always has been. Most of his work displays wild flowers from the temperate zone for the most part, although he has been known to go much farther afield. It is not that he travels to find inspiration; he says he'll never run out of ideas found on his land. But he does have a passion for orchids, and these do appear in his work. Even for these he need not go farther than the hothouses of Longwood Gardens in nearby Pennsylvania, where he can sketch orchids.

Whatever the frustrations, whatever the inherent limitations of working in the tradition he does, Paul Stankard is proud of being, as he puts it, an artist-craftsperson who works with glass. He knows that some people will relegate him to the realm of artisan, because his work doesn't smack of the new, but this seems to amuse him more than anything. He realizes that there is no other medium that could capture what he's trying to do, not stone, not bronze, not clay. There is a permanence, an eternal quality that appeals to him, that compensates for the restrictions of the medium. What he accomplishes with his flame can only be done in glass. The fragility and impermanence of a wild blossom become permanent. Like a Jurassic insect trapped in amber, his flowers will still be blooming, still be fresh and bright, decades, centuries from now. Someday, as Paul sees it, there may not be meadows full of wild flowers anywhere. People may have to learn to appreciate Nature's beauty on a more intimate level, because the grandeur of Nature will have been destroyed. Sad as this vision is, Paul feels that his work anticipates that kind of intimate experience of Nature. His work will keep his sense of wonder alive long after he is gone.

Competition with the past is a significant motivation in Paul's studio, and has been since his earliest successes. "I want to be better than Clichy and Saint-Louis and Baccarat." He also wants to be better than himself. Although not apparent in the short term, change is very clear over time in his work. This constant evolution is necessary, both to keep his interest going and to keep his artistic vision alive. Without constant new challenges to be met at the bench, without new problems to solve, Paul's work would wither and die like the plants he depicts. Recently Paul has returned to producing paperweights. Shunted aside by the botanicals in 1990, they have come back, both as valid art forms, and as studies for the botanicals. Paperweights also are a way to make his work more accessible to a wider audience. The breadth of Paul's marketplace is, of course, a practical consideration, but also an emotional one. The more people who can see and own his work, the more people he can give his message to. A friend once teased him that the only person whose understanding of flowers or Nature is expanded by his work is himself. But for Paul, the chance that someone might be moved by his work, might see Nature the way he sees it, is always there.

Part of his competition with the past can be seen in his teaching. In a delicious bit of historic irony, he is presently teaching courses in lampwork and glassblowing at Rowan College in South Jersey, and is fully committed to his job. "If you're going to have any sort of integrity as a teacher, you can't keep any secrets," he declares. This is not a new concept for him. Paul was the first artist in the history of paperweights to do public demonstrations, to pull the veil of secrecy from his work. In 1986 he made a paperweight before a large, enthusiastic audience at Wheaton Village, a popular museum in Millville, New

Jersey. Later that same year he ran a five-day workshop at the Penland School of Crafts in North Carolina, sharing and explaining every detail of the process that had made him famous. Imagine a celebrated magician giving away all of his tricks, and you can imagine the enormity of Paul's generosity. Many in his audience were professional glass artists, just those people who, with their art training and drive for originality, might be inclined to think of Paul as a mere artisan. They all spent many hours that week, sometimes until four in the morning, trying to do what Paul had shown them. Few people can watch him work and not fall under his spell.

At Wheaton, during the 1995 Glass Weekend (organized by Wheaton's offspring, the Creative Glass Center of America, of which Paul is a trustee and past board president), a carnival atmosphere prevailed during his morning-long demonstration before an audience of glass collectors, curators, and glass artists. Only the lack of a calliope in the background prevented it entirely from seeming like a boisterous sideshow. A huge vase of wild flowers at his side for inspiration, his casual and fluent patter was astonishing. As he made petals and leaves for black-eyed Susans, he talked about the work of other glass artists he admired, in particular about Dante Marioni and Richard Marquis, two Seattle-based artists who were working with him at the furnace that day. He was as lavish with his praise as with his information. One highlight came as he prepared a male earth spirit figure for his paperweight. Speaking of another artist present that weekend, Lucio Bubacco, a Venetian lampworker born in Murano, Paul commented that "Lucio gave me the courage to put penises on my root people." Not only did this delight the audience, but it typified Paul's willingness to acknowledge other artists' influence on his work. Remembering the hard-won skills and practice of two decades makes his ability to talk and work somewhat less amazing, but his willingness to share, to promote others, still makes one marvel.

Intellectual generosity is just part of another legacy Paul hopes to leave. His assistants, Christine and David, are also part of that legacy. He wants to pass on the love of lampwork that brought him where he is today. He wants the magic that turned him into an artist, and the passion that kept him working, to be passed on to the next generation. At fifty-two, Paul is conscious that he has, if he's lucky, twenty years left at the bench. He can get bored with his work; his fingers get stiff, he has aches and pains that come with age. In his daughter Christine, in his assistant David, and in all the people he reaches with his demonstrations and his teaching, Paul sees the future.

TOP: *St. Anthony's Fire.* 1976. Engraved: 02876; D. 3".
Diorio Collection. MIDDLE: *Compound Chokeberry.*
1977. Engraved: 43877; D. 3". Diorio Collection.
BOTTOM: *Black-Eyed Susan.* 1979. Engraved:
A978; D. 3¼". Diorio Collection

OPPOSITE, CLOCKWISE, FROM THE TOP: *Red Plantain.* 1974. Engraved:
A565 13/50; D. 2½". Diorio Collection; *Forget-Me-Not.* 1974.
Engraved: 4C-A506; D. 2½". Diorio Collection; *Brandywine Fall
Bouquet.* 1979. Engraved: A975; D. 3¼". Diorio Collection;
Goat's Rue. 1974. Engraved: A76; D. 2½". Diorio Collection
*The Brandywine was the first paperweight to use a seasonal
theme, combining dried flowers with seedpods and berries.*

Top left: *Faceted Smithsonian Issued Wild Rose.* 1978. Engraved: B123; D. 2¾". Limited edition. Diorio Collection. Middle: *Faceted Yellow Meadow Wreath.* 1974. Engraved: D402, S initial cane; D. 2¾". Diorio Collection. Bottom: *Faceted Yellow Stylized Flower.* 1979. Engraved: D402; D. 2¾". Diorio Collection
The wild rose was issued as a limited edition for the Smithsonian in Washington, D.C.

Opposite, clockwise, from top right: *Peach Blossom Scent Bottle.* 1981. Engraved: D101; H. 4¾", D. 2½". Diorio Collection; *Compound Trillium.* 1974. Engraved: D084; D. 2½". Diorio Collection; *Faceted Stylized Flower on Blue Ground.* n.d.; D. 2⁹⁄₁₆". Belkin Collection; *Faceted Wild Roses with Rose Hips.* 1985. Engraved: Experimental A37, PS initial cane; D. 3". Belkin Collection; *Faceted Red Maid Footed Paperweight.* 1973. Engraved: 424, PS initial cane; wheel cut; H. 2½". Belkin Collection; *Upright Multi-faceted Rose Botanical Paperweight.* 1982. Engraved: D124; H. 3½", W. 2¼". Diorio Collection
This group was among the earliest of Stankard's paperweights; the peach blossom was the only bottle-and-stopper he made, and the stylized blue flower among his first.

LEFT TO RIGHT: *Clintonia Botanical* (and underside detail). 1981. Engraved: Paul J. Stankard D099; H. 3". Diorio Collection;
Stylized Mottled Flower Botanical. 1983. Engraved: Paul J. Stankard H42; H. 3⅞". Belkin Collection;
Botanical Loosestrife. 1981. Engraved: 35; H. 3⅞". Diorio Collection
Shown at right, the loosestrife botanical was the artist's first experimental botanical.

TOP: *Cattleya Orchid.* 1974. Engraved:
A736; D. 2½". Diorio Collection.
MIDDLE: *Bellwort.* 1974. Engraved: A537
18/75; D. 2½". Diorio Collection.
BOTTOM: *Flax on Green Ground.* 1980.
Engraved: A102; D. 3⅛". Diorio Collection

ABOVE: *Dwarf Field Pansy.* 1978. Engraved: A740;
D. 3". Diorio Collection. BELOW: *Bloodroot.* 1981.
Engraved: D501; D. 3". Diorio Collection
*Seeds appeared for the first time in the pansy
weight, suggesting the life cycle of a plant.*

Opposite, near right: *Gentians with Earth Clump and Golden Bowl* (and detail). 1989. Engraved: Especially for Pat Love, Paul; H. 4". Stankard Collection. Opposite, far right: *Cloistered Pine Barren Bouquet Botanical with Golden Bowl and Earth Spirits*. 1989. Engraved: Paul J. Stankard E20; H. 4¾". Belkin Collection

Blue-Eyed Grass. 1982. Engraved: D115; D. 3⅛". Diorio Collection
The full life cycle of the plant—bud, blossom, and pod—appears here.

Bottle Gentian (Closed Blossoms). 1981. Engraved: B414; D. 3⅛". Diorio Collection
Note the blossom made in cross section at the lower left.

Compound Wood Violets.
1978. Engraved: B07; D 2¾".
Diorio Collection

Botanical Interpretation.
1978. Engraved: A742;
D. 2¾". Diorio Collection

Opposite: *Compound Lilacs.*
1979. Engraved: A733; D. 3".
Diorio Collection
*The complex lilac blossoms
were the most ambitious
flowers attempted in the 1970s.*

BERRY PROCESS *Sepals and a stem of brown-cased green glass are added to the back of a finished berry.*

ABOVE: *Blackberry Bouquet.* 1979. Engraved: A745 13/75; D. 3". Diorio Collection.
BELOW: *Sippiwisset Bouquet.* 1979. Engraved: A419; D. 3". Diorio Collection

ABOVE: *Bloodroot.* 1981. Engraved: experimental B265;
D. 3". Belkin Collection. BELOW: *Mountain Hawthorn.*
1983. Engraved: B1005; D. 3⅛". Diorio Collection.
The hawthorn blossoms were the first that Stankard
designed to be seen equally from above or below.

Clockwise, from the top: *Epiphytic Orchid.* 1982. Engraved: B593; D. 3¼". Diorio Collection; *Wilted Meadow Wreath.* 1981. Engraved: D812; D. 3". Diorio Collection; *Wilted Spring Beauty.* 1981. Engraved: D811; D. 3⅛". Diorio Collection

Pink Lady's Slipper on Blue Ground. 1983.
Engraved: D137; D. 3". Diorio Collection

Paphiopedilum Orchid with Anthropomorphic Roots on Green Ground.
1991. Engraved: Paul J. Stankard C53; D. 3⁵⁄₁₆". Belkin Collection

Compound Showy Lady's Slipper. 1979. Engraved: A832; D. 3½". Diorio Collection

PAGES 70–71: *Paphiopedilum Orchid Botanical* (and detail). 1991. Engraved: B21;
H. 5⅞", W. 3". Diorio Collection. *Ophry Orchid Botanical with Bees.* 1992.
Engraved: Paul J. Stankard D5; H. 5½". Belkin Collection

ORCHID PROCESS *The leaves, roots, and pseudobulb of an orchid are melted and then affixed to the blossom in order to create an entire plant. Tweezers support a leaf of cased brown and green glass until its joint cools and becomes stable. At left, a finished cattleya orchid, soon to be removed from the glass supporting rod, will be encased in molten crystal.*

TOP RIGHT: *Cymbidium Orchid*. 1993. Engraved: F19, PS/93 initial cane; D. 3⅛". Belkin Collection.
MIDDLE: *Compound Phalenopsis Orchid*. 1982. Engraved: B592; D. 3¼". Diorio Collection.
BOTTOM RIGHT: *Catteleya Orchid*. 1992. Engraved: Especially for Annie Love Pat and Paul 6/16/92; D. 3¼". Belkin Collection
Metallic enamels were used to create the colored details and markings of the cymbidium orchid.

Wedding Trillium Bouquet. 1980. Engraved: D809; D. 3½". Diorio Collection
Instead of a traditional floral bouquet, a young bride carried a glass bouquet similar to this one.

Opposite, top left: *Chicago Art Institute's Spring Beauty Bouquet.* 1979. Engraved: D731;
D. 3". Diorio Collection. Middle: *Orchid Bouquet.* 1981. Engraved: D098 Stankard 1981.
Limited edition of 25; D. 3". Diorio Collection. Bottom: *Compound Apple Blossoms.*
1980. Engraved: A134. Limited edition of 25; D. 3⅜". Diorio Collection

Detail from above, *Pine Barren Gentians Botanical Cube*

Detail from above, *Coronet Bouquet Botanical Cube*

Opposite, left: *Pine Barren Gentians Botanical Cube.* 1988. Engraved: Paul J. Stankard A26; H. 2½". Belkin Collection. Right: *Coronet Bouquet Botanical Cube.* 1995. Engraved: Paul J. Stankard F62; H. 3½". Belkin Collection

Lilac Cloistered Botanical (and detail). 1991. Engraved: Paul J. Stankard A38; H. 6". Pilloff Collection

Braided Bouquet. 1982. Engraved: D502; D. 2⅞". Diorio Collection

Opposite: *Cloistered Daisy Botanical.* 1993. Engraved: E14; H. 6".
Stankard Collection

ABOVE: *Arbutus Bouquet.* 1985. S initial cane; D. 3⅜". Stankard Collection. BELOW: *Arbutus Bouquet with Raspberries.* 1986. Engraved: Paul J. Stankard A177; D. 3⅜". Belkin Collection

OPPOSITE, TOP: *Bouquet.* 1978. Engraved: B121, red S initial cane; D. 2⅞". Diorio Collection.
MIDDLE: *Summer Field Arrangement.* n.d. Limited edition of 25; D. 3". Stankard Collection.
BOTTOM: *Pine Barren Arbutus Bouquet.* 1986. Engraved: D503; D. 3½". Diorio Collection
A vacation in Maine inspired Summer Field Arrangement.

ABOVE: *White Tea Rose.* 1979. Engraved: Experimental D401; D. 2". Diorio Collection.
BELOW: *Red Tea Rose.* 1984. Engraved: A180, S initial cane; D. 2". Belkin Collection
Spink & Sons, London, commissioned the white rose design for the Queen Mother's
80th birthday, which they presented to her as a birthday gift.

OPPOSITE: *Summer Field Arrangement.* 1977. Engraved: 43077; D. 3". Diorio Collection

OPPOSITE: *Bouquet Botanical* (and detail). 1989. Engraved:
Paul J. Stankard E63; H. 5½". Belkin Collection
Note the gold leaf fragments in the detail.

PAGES 88–89: *Coronet with Red Damselfly, Honeybee and Spirit Cluster* (and
details). 1995. Engraved: Paul J. Stankard B65; H. 4½". Belkin Collection

DAMSELFLY PROCESS *Various components of a damselfly such as the wings, thorax, head, legs, and abdomen are sculpted from thin drawn rods of colored and colorless glass. Then the bits and pieces are assembled one at a time. First the body is made by sealing each of its three parts: the heat of the flame melts each part just enough to fuse it to its mate. The bracing structure of the thread-thin legs helps to hold them in position. The wings are the last parts attached and positioned while still hot. The finished damselfly—it is made in red, blue, or green—is still attached to the support rod, which will be removed later on.*

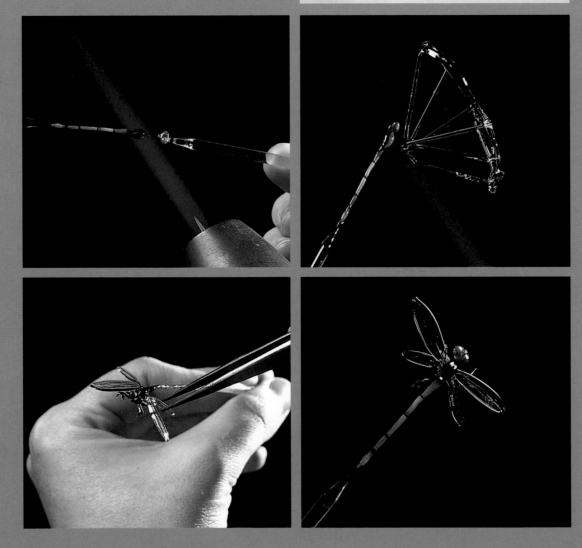

Coronets, Blueberries, and Damselflies. 1995. Engraved: Paul J.
Stankard F56, PS/95 initial cane; D. 3⁵⁄₁₆". Belkin Collection

Morning Glory. 1984. Engraved: D490; D. 3". Diorio Collection

Opposite, top: *Blue Morning Glory.* 1984. Engraved: D494; D. 3¼". Diorio Collection.
Middle: *Cayenne Pepper.* 1974. Engraved: A573; D. 2½". Diorio Collection.
Bottom: *Pink-Striped Morning Glory.* 1984. Engraved: A618; D. 3". Diorio Collection
*The coiled stem of the pepper plant allowed for a much looser design
than the traditional paperweight format offered.*

OPPOSITE: *Cymbidium Orchid on Blue Ground.* 1993. Engraved: T38, PS/93 initial cane; D. 3⁵⁄₁₆". Belkin Collection
Metallic oxide enamels were used to create the red details.

TOP LEFT: *Lily of the Valley.* 1984. Engraved: Experimental A-103; D. 3". Diorio Collection. MIDDLE: *Medieval Herbal.* 1979. Engraved: A540; D. 3". Diorio Collection.
LEFT: *Mountain Laurel on Blue Ground.* 1991. Engraved: Paul J. Stankard B57; D. 3⅜". Belkin Collection
The mountain laurel remains the artist's most ambitious blossom to date. This example was his first successful effort. Similarly, the human form in the roots shown above have become a signature of the artist's style.

Goatsbeard Daisy Bouquet Cloistered Botanical (and detail). 1989. Engraved: Paul J. Stankard F19; H. 6½". Belkin Collection

Bouquet Cloistered Botanical. 1990. Engraved: Especially for Pat, Love Paul; H. 6". Stankard Collection

Spring Beauty Cloistered Botanical (and detail). 1988. Engraved: D186; H. 6". Diorio Collection
An especially ambitious and complex botanical, this shows the varied iconography and layered structure of the largest pieces.

Pink Lady's Slipper Botanical. 1984. Engraved: Paul J. Stankard 69; H. 4". Belkin Collection

Opposite: *Lady's Slipper Botanical with Bulbous Form Entwined in Roots.* 1989. Engraved: E84 1989; H. 5⅝".
Collection The Huntington Museum of Art, West Virginia

TOP: *Brassi Diorii Stylized Orchid.* 1982. Engraved: D125; D. 3". Diorio Collection. MIDDLE: *Moccasin Flower, Pink Lady's Slipper.* 1983. Engraved: D130; D. 3". Diorio Collection. BOTTOM: *Paphiopedilum Orchid.* 1989. Engraved: Paul J. Stankard EGW2; D. 3⅛". Belkin Collection

Braided Blackberry Bouquet (and detail). 1983.
Engraved: B1004; D. 3⅛". Diorio Collection

Water Lily. 1987. Engraved: D–184; D. 3¼". Diorio Collection
*A careful look at the underside, shown opposite, detects
the hidden water spirits, which are tinted green because
of their aquatic environment.*

Water Lily. 1990. Engraved: Paul J. Stankard B26;
D. 3³⁄₁₆". Belkin Collection

Indian Squash Gourds with Warts. 1986. Engraved:
C195, S initial cane; D. 3⁵⁄₁₆". Belkin Collection

Opposite: *Indian Squash Gourds with Warts.* 1986.
Engraved: S initial cane; D. 3⁵⁄₁₆". Diorio Collection

OPPOSITE, TOP: *Spirits Environmental.* 1993. Engraved: Paul J. Stankard D38; D. 3¼". Belkin Collection. MIDDLE LEFT AND DETAIL, PAGE 112: *Environmental with Turtle.* 1995. Engraved: Collaboration with Rick Ayotte F66; D. 3¼". Belkin Collection. MIDDLE RIGHT AND DETAIL, PAGE 113: *Red Prickly Pear Cactus Environmental.* 1985; D. 3". Diorio Collection. BOTTOM: *Environmental.* 1984; D. 3¼". Diorio Collection *Various shades of ground brown glass were used to create the feeling of sandy soil as seen in the work at top.*

Detail, *Environmental*

OPPOSITE: Detail, *Red Prickly Pear Cactus Environmental*

RASPBERRY PROCESS *A small red blob of glass is the basis for a raspberry. Onto its surface tiny red droplets are added one by one—hot enough to seal together without being so hot as to lose their shape. Using a predrawn rod of red glass the right size makes this process easier, until the completed fruit is ready to get leaves and sepals.*

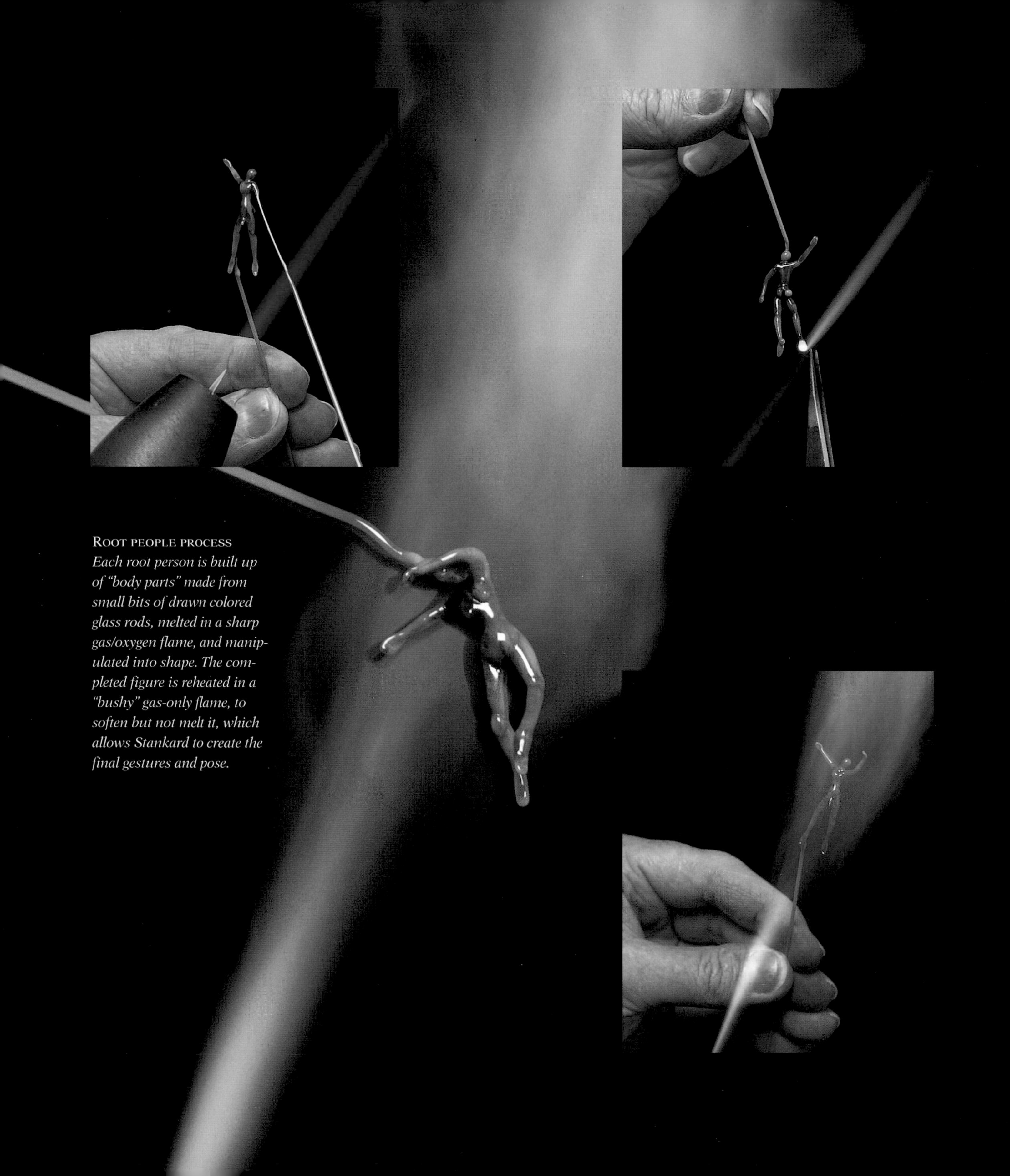

ROOT PEOPLE PROCESS
*Each root person is built up
of "body parts" made from
small bits of drawn colored
glass rods, melted in a sharp
gas/oxygen flame, and manipulated into shape. The completed figure is reheated in a
"bushy" gas-only flame, to
soften but not melt it, which
allows Stankard to create the
final gestures and pose.*

ABOVE: *Bindweed and Forget-Me-Not Environmental.* 1992. Engraved:
Paul J. Stankard B12; D. 3⅜". Belkin Collection. BELOW: Underside
detail of *Under the Earth: Spirits.* 1994. Engraved: Paul J.
Stankard W26, PS/94 initial cane; D. 3⁵⁄₁₆". Belkin Collection
*Five shades of crushed brown glass make up the
sandy soil of the environmental paperweights.*

YELLOW FLOWER [CORONET] PROCESS *To make the coronet, one of Stankard's fictionalized blossoms, a cluster of slender stamens is sealed on a dot of yellow glass. Red-hot petals, formed of yellow glass cased with white for a natural translucence, are applied to the crown and manipulated to give each flower a unique character. Using tweezers, a red-hot bud is carefully applied to an adjacent stem.*

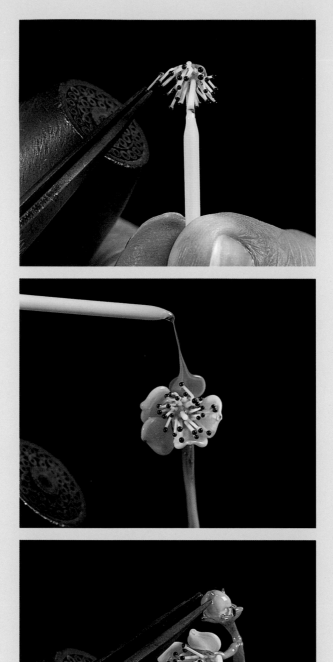

OPPOSITE, TOP LEFT: *Asiatic Dayflower.* 1994. Engraved: Paul J. Stankard W41, PS/94 initial cane; D. 3¼". Belkin Collection. TOP RIGHT: *Coronet with Spirit.* 1994. Engraved: Paul J. Stankard S79, PS/94 initial cane; D. 3¼". Stankard Collection. BOTTOM: *Goatsbeard.* 1989. Engraved: Paul J. Stankard B12; D. 3⁵⁄₁₆". Belkin Collection
The Asiatic dayflower is common to southern New Jersey, the artist's homeland. When making this wild flower the artist learned that slender stamens would not crumple in the heat of the molten crystal.

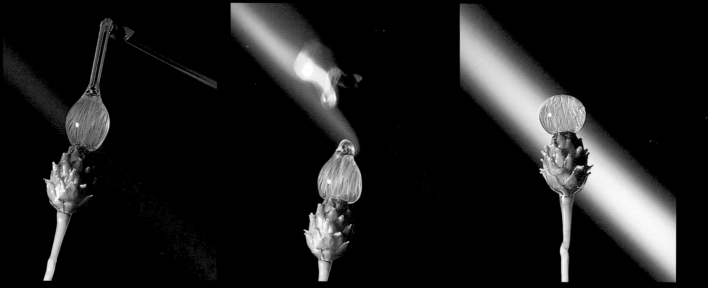

THISTLE PROCESS *Building a thistle blossom begins with a dense cluster of fine, hairlike, lavender glass rods, encased in colorless crystal to create the "tusk" of the plant. This tusk is then applied to the sepals and rounded off in the flame. When encased in the botanical block, the tusk's lavender stamens appear to stand alone.*

TOP: *Common Mullein with Honeybee.* 1992. Engraved: C5392; D. 3¼".
Diorio Collection. MIDDLE: *Thistle.* 1990. Engraved: Paul J. Stankard B3;
D. 3⅛". Belkin Collection. BOTTOM AND DETAIL, OPPOSITE: *Indian Pipes.* 1995.
Engraved: Paul J. Stankard S34, PS/94 initial cane; D. 3⅛". Belkin Collection

OPPOSITE: *Autumn Bouquet Cloistered Botanical* (and detail). n.d. Engraved: Paul J. Stankard B19; H. 5¾". Belkin Collection
The translucent pod beneath the bouquet allows the red seeds within to show, taking full advantage of glass as a medium.

Rose Bouquet Botanical (and detail). 1992. Engraved: Paul J. Stankard C2; H. 4¼". Pilloff Collection

Underside detail, *Mountain Laurel Bouquet with Blackberries*

ABOVE: *Bouquet with Unripe Blackberry.* 1991. Engraved: Paul J. Stankard C27; D. 3⅝". Belkin Collection.
BELOW: *Mountain Laurel Bouquet with Blackberries*. 1993. Engraved: F51, PS/93 initial cane; 3¼". Belkin Collection

Hive Bouquet with Black-Eyed Susans and Blueberries (and detail). 1994; D. 3¼". Diorio Collection
Here the honeycomb has been placed in an impossible context, but one that looks credible nonetheless.

Top: *Honeybee Hive Bouquet,* 1993. Engraved: Paul J. Stankard A9; D. 3⁵⁄₁₆". Belkin Collection. Middle: *Honeybee Hive Bouquet.* 1993. Engraved: F57, PS/93 initial cane; D. 3⁵⁄₁₆". Belkin Collection. Bottom: *Paper Wasp Hive Bouquet.* 1993. Engraved: Paul J. Stankard A14 To Pat, Love Paul 1; D. 3⁵⁄₁₆". Stankard Collection

TOP: *Honeybee Hive Bouquet*. 1995. Engraved:
S94, PS/95 initial cane; D. 3¼". Diorio Collection.
MIDDLE AND DETAIL, PAGE 130: *Honeybee Hive Bouquet*.
1993. Engraved: A10-93; D. 3¼". Diorio Collection.
BOTTOM AND DETAIL, PAGE 131: *Honeybee Hive Bouquet*.
1994. Engraved: Paul J. Stankard S96, PS/95
initial cane; D. 3⅜". Belkin Collection

Underside detail, *Honeybee Hive Bouquet.* 1993

<small>Opposite:</small> Detail, *Honeybee Hive Bouquet.* 1994

Honeycomb Bouquet with Worker Bees. 1993. Engraved: F67; D. 3⁵⁄₁₆". Stankard Collection

Opposite: *Mountain Laurel Botanical.* 1994. Engraved: Paul J. Stankard B25; H. 5".
Belkin Collection

MOUNTAIN LAUREL PROCESS *In making a mountain laurel sprig, the crown of stamens is first assembled, then encased in a crystal sphere, which is shaped while hot to mimic the form of the blossom. Using thin rods of white glass, the hinged flower is gradually assembled; tweezers manipulate the white glass, sculpting it into the familiar ridges of the blossom. Rods of brown-cased green glass are used for the sepals and stem, completing a single blossom. The hot plate keeps blossoms, buds, and leaves workable as they are sealed onto a branch to create a cluster. The assembled cluster is then manipulated with tweezers into its final form and set aside to await its ultimate encasement in molten crystal.*

LEFT: *Mountain Laurel Bouquet Botanical Cube.* 1995. Engraved: Paul J. Stankard F33; H. 3⅛". Pilloff Collection.
RIGHT: *Bouquet Botanical Cube with Honeybee.* 1992. Engraved: Paul J. Stankard C59; H. 3⅞". Belkin Collection

OPPOSITE: *Mountain Laurel Diptych Botanical* (and detail). 1994.
Engraved: Paul J. Stankard C10-94; H. 5¾". Diorio Collection
*Note the honeybee in the mountain laurel blossom. The diptych
botanicals are laminated together after they are cut and polished.*

Deptford Pink Cloistered Botanical (and detail). 1986. Engraved: Paul J. Stankard C28; H. 5½". Belkin Collection
The detail shows an "earth flower," which represents the unseen miracles of life and growth.

OPPOSITE: *Spring's Beauty, Terrestrial Light Botanical* (and detail). 1992. Engraved: Paul J. Stankard B5; H. 6½". Pilloff Collection
Pollen sacks can be seen on the honeybee's rear legs.

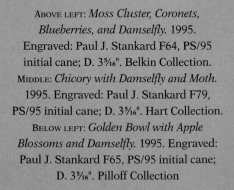

ABOVE LEFT: *Moss Cluster, Coronets,*
Blueberries, and Damselfly. 1995.
Engraved: Paul J. Stankard F64, PS/95
initial cane; D. 3⁵⁄₁₆". Belkin Collection.
MIDDLE: *Chicory with Damselfly and Moth.*
1995. Engraved: Paul J. Stankard F79,
PS/95 initial cane; D. 3⁵⁄₁₆". Hart Collection.
BELOW LEFT: *Golden Bowl with Apple*
Blossoms and Damselfly. 1995. Engraved:
Paul J. Stankard F65, PS/95 initial cane;
D. 3⁵⁄₁₆". Pilloff Collection

ABOVE: *Apple Blossoms, Blueberries and Blue Damselfly with Golden Bowl.* 1995. Engraved: Paul J. Stankard F79, PS/95 initial cane; D. 3⁵⁄₁₆". Stankard Collection.

BELOW AND DETAIL, PAGE 145: *Raspberries, Forget-Me-Nots, and Damselfly with Golden Bowl.* 1995. Engraved: Paul J. Stankard F29, PS/95 initial cane; D. 3¼". Belkin Collection

WORD CANES *The actual word cane mosaic is built by Stankard, who individually forms each letter. The mosaic letters are then bundled and redrawn to form one word, at which point they are nearly an inch wide. After repeated drawing, the final size of the word canes is about ⅛" across. Intended to be read with a magnifying glass in his work, the artist's full vocabulary includes* wet, pollen, scent, seeds, fertile, you, *and* terra.

OPPOSITE: Underside detail, *Raspberries, Forget-Me-Nots, and Damselfly with Golden Bowl*

OPPOSITE AND DETAILS, ABOVE AND PAGES 148–49: *Blackberry and Coronet Diptych with Golden Bowl and Honeybees*. 1995.
Engraved: D2 1995; H. 6". Collection Dr. and Mrs. Millo, France

OPPOSITE: *Desert's Still Time, Diptych Botanical* (and detail). 1993. Engraved: Paul J. Stankard C5; H. 6". Belkin Collection
A diptych such as this requires as many pick-ups of hot glass as eight paperweights.

OPPOSITE: *Coronet Botanical Cube* (and detail). 1995. Engraved: Paul J. Stankard F1; H. 5¼". Belkin Collection

PAGES 154–55: *September Seeds, Triptych Botanical* (and details). 1992. Engraved: Paul J. Stankard B9; H. 5¾". Pilloff Collection
The seasonal cycle is portrayed in this large-scale triptych.

1943   Born April 7 in North Attleboro, Massachusetts

1957   Graduates St. Mary's Parochial School and begins high school in North Attleboro

1958   The Stankard family moves to Wenonah, New Jersey

1961   Graduates Pitman High School, Pitman, New Jersey; enters the glassblowing program at Salem County Vocational Technical Institute (now Salem County Community College), New Jersey

1962   Takes first summer job as a full-time glassblower

1963   Receives a diploma in Scientific Glassblowing Technology from Salem County Vocational Technical Institute

Meets Francis Whittemore, celebrated lampworker

Works for McAllister Scientific in Nashua, New Hampshire, as a production glassblower

Meets and works with Roland Ayotte, who would become a lifelong friend

Works for Fisher Scientific in New York City

1964   May 2: Marries Patricia Ann LaPatrick of Deptford, New Jersey, a secretary in the Engineering Department at Campbell Soup in Camden, New Jersey

Works for Andrews Glass Company in Vineland, New Jersey (a division of Fischer Porter, Incorporated) as a production glassblower

1965   Begins to produce glass animal novelties part-time, selling them for 35 cents each to supplement family income

December: First child, Christine, is born

1966   Works for S. & J. Industries, Alexandria, Virginia, as an Advanced Glass Instrument Glassblower

1967   Works for Philco-Ford Company, Electron Optical Division, Spring City, Pennsylvania, making precision glass-to-metal seals and precision glass instruments

May: Second child, Pauline, is born

1969   Works for Rohm & Haas, Philadelphia, in charge of Research Glassblowing facilities

Abandons glass animals to concentrate on making paperweights

May: Third child, Katherine, is born

1970   Meets Arthur Gorham at his paperweight shop in Millville, New Jersey; also meets antique paperweight dealers Theresa and Arthur Greenblatt

1971   Sells first paperweights for $20

Included in an exhibition on South Jersey glass at The New Jersey State Museum, Trenton

Establishes relationship with Larry Selman, a paperweight dealer in Santa Cruz, California

Reese Palley, Atlantic City gallery owner, discovers Stankard's paperweights in Walter LaPatrick's booth at the Indian Summer Art Show on the boardwalk in Atlantic City

December: Palley includes Stankard in a group show in his gallery; all the works sell

1972   January: Fourth child, Joseph, is born

At Palley's urging, Stankard leaves his full-time job at Rohm & Haas to devote his career to making paperweights

Meets Jack Feingold of Gem Antiques, New York City

1973   Attends a paperweight conference in Chicago, where he meets Paul Rubuloff, prominent paperweight collector

Clears $6,000 his first year on his own

1974   Meets Leo, Ruth, Allan and Suzy Kaplan, of Leo Kaplan, Inc., New York City

Clears $7,200 his second year

1975   Meets Michael Diorio, nature photographer and dentist

Meets glass artist Tom Patti, who works in small scale

Hires John Glass, his first assistant

Remortgages his house to buy 5,000 pounds of fine soda-lime crystal for $15,000

Attends a paperweight conference in Washington, D.C., where his work is being exhibited at the Smithsonian Institution

Attends a symposium on contemporary glass at the Bergstrom-Mahler Museum in Neenah, Wisconsin, where he first meets Dominick Labino and Harvey Littleton

Before his death, Martin Francis Stankard, Paul's father, donates two paperweights to the Smithsonian Institution's National Museum of American Art, at their request

1977   Produces the first of a series of limited-edition paperweights for the Smithsonian Institution

1978   Group exhibition: "Great Paperweight Exhibit," Habatat Gallery, Pontiac, Michigan

Group exhibition: "Paperweights: Flowers Which Clothe the Meadows," paperweight exhibition, The Corning Museum of Glass, Corning, New York

1979   First one-man exhibition at The Contemporary Art Glass Gallery (now the Heller Gallery), New York City; all works sell

Rejected for the 1979 "New Glass Review," The Corning Museum of Glass

Begins experimenting with a new form to present wild flowers

Sees the exhibition "The Courage to Create" at the Franklin Institute, Philadelphia

"Paul Stankard: The First Decade" opens at the Museum of American Glass at Wheaton Village, Millville, New Jersey

1980   With Wheaton Village's director, Barry Taylor, begins to establish the Creative Glass Center of America

Attends and lectures at The Corning Glass Seminar on paperweights

Hires Jim Donofrio

Produces his first experimental botanical sculptures

1981   Included in "Flora in Glass" exhibition, Spink & Son, London

1982   October: Fifth child, Philip, is born

Produces a series of limited-edition paperweights for the Art Institute of Chicago

"Nature Translated in Glass: Paperweights and Botanicals by Paul Stankard," The New Jersey State Museum, Trenton

Root people begin to appear in the paperweights and botanicals

1984   Becomes a founding board member of the Creative Glass Center of America, at Wheaton Village in Millville

Meets Mike Belkin, prominent paperweight collector

1985   With David Lewin, develops the cloistered botanical form

1986   Receives the New Jersey State Council on the Arts Award for Excellence

Establishes the first flameworking studio at the Penland School of Crafts in Penland, North Carolina

Group exhibition: "Flowers from Flame," Museum of American Glass, Wheaton Village, Millville, New Jersey

1987   Teaches summer session at Penland School of Crafts

1988   Group exhibition: "World Glass Now," Hokkaido Museum of Modern Art, Sapporo, Japan

Becomes president of the board of the Creative Glass Center of America

Begins sending work to glass cutter Dennis Gentile

1989   Receives a second New Jersey State Council on the Arts

Award for Excellence

"Paul Stankard: Nature in Glass," Pennsylvania
Horticultural Society, Philadelphia

Teaches flameworking at the Pilchuck Glass School,
Seattle

"Paul Stankard: A Twenty-Year Retrospective,"
Museum of American Glass, Wheaton Village,
Millville, New Jersey

Video, "Nature in Glass: The Private World of Paul
Stankard," Paperweight Press

Hires David Graeber

1990   "Paul Stankard's Botanicals," Longwood Gardens,
Kennett Square, Pennsylvania

"Paul Stankard: Nature in Glass and Verse," The
Morris Museum of Arts and Sciences, Morristown,
New Jersey

Included in "Masterpieces of American Glass," based
on collections of The Corning Museum of Glass and
The Toledo Museum of Art, which travels throughout
the Soviet Union

1990, 1991, 1993   Teaches flameworking at the Penland School
of Craft, Penland, North Carolina

1991   One-man show at the New Orleans School of GlassWorks
and Gallery

Technical adviser for "Nature's Wonders in Glass: The
Arts of the Blaschkas," The Corning Museum of
Glass

Inducted into the Millville Rose Society of the
Wheaton Cultural Alliance

Elected as a Fellow of The Corning Museum of Glass

1992   Receives a High Merit Award in the "International
Exhibition of Glass Kanazawa '92," Ishikawa
Exhibition Hall, Kanazawa, Japan

Group exhibition: "A Decade of Craft," American Craft
Museum, New York

Group exhibition: "International Contemporary Glass
Exhibition," Rufino Tamayo Museum, Mexico City

Commission from Mobil Corporation to make a wild

flower botanical sculpture for the Indonesian
Minister of Science

Included in "Treasures from The Corning Museum of
Glass," Yokohama Museum of Art, Yokohama, Japan

Christine Stankard begins working with her father

1993   Video, "American Craftsman: Paul J. Stankard," NHK
Enterprises, Public Television, Tokyo, Japan

Receives Excellence Award from the New Jersey
Council of County Colleges

"Paul Stankard: Master of the Flame," Contemporary
Craft Gallery at The Newark Museum, to commemo-
rate his fiftieth birthday

Group exhibition: "Maximizing the Minimum: Small
Glass Sculpture," Museum of American Glass,
Wheaton Village, Millville, New Jersey

1994   "Nature in Glass," Singapore Pools, Ltd., the state-owned
lottery company of Singapore

Video, "Laborare Est Orare: By Paul Stankard," Art
Glass Association of Southern California

Begins working with glass artist Steve Weinberg on
kiln-cast botanicals

1995   Lloyd Herman, former curator of the Renwick Gallery
of the National Museum of American Art, selects
Stankard's work for inclusion in "American Glass:
Masters of the Art." The show, focusing on 10–12
leaders in the contemporary glass field, is sponsored
by the United States Information Agency, and will
travel through Europe in 1996 and 1997

Group exhibition: "Contemporary Glass Exhibition
'95," Hisinchu Cultural Center, Hisinchu, Taiwan;
also at the "Contemporary Glass Exhibition," Taipei,
Taiwan

Group exhibition: "International Survey of Contemporary Art Glass," organized by the Pittsburgh Cultural
Trust and Concept Art Gallery, Pittsburgh

Visiting Professor of Flameworking, Rowan College,
Glassboro, New Jersey

Public Collections

American Craft Museum, New York
Art Institute of Chicago
Asheville Art Museum, North Carolina
Bergstrom-Mahler Museum, Neenah, Wisconsin
Brooklyn Museum
Chrysler Museum, Norfolk, Virginia
Cleveland Museum of Art
The Corning Museum of Glass, Corning, New York
GlasMuseum, Elbeltoft, Denmark
Hokkaido Museum of Modern Art, Sapporo, Japan
Huntington Museum of Art, Huntington, West Virginia
Indianapolis Museum of Art
The J.B. Speed Art Museum, Louisville, Kentucky
The Metropolitan Museum of Art, New York
Milwaukee Art Museum
Milwaukee Public Museum
Missouri Botanical Garden, St. Louis
Morris Museum of Arts and Sciences, Morristown, New Jersey
Musée des Arts Décoratifs, Paris
Museum of American Glass, Wheaton Village, Millville, New Jersey
Museum of Fine Arts, Boston, Massachusetts
National Museum of American Art, Renwick Gallery, Washington, D.C.
National Museum of American Art, Smithsonian Institution, Washington, D.C.
The Newark Museum
The New Jersey State Museum, Trenton
New Orleans Museum of Art
Philadelphia Museum of Art
Pilchuck Collection, Stanwood, Washington
Royal Ontario Museum, Toronto
The Sandwich Historical Society Glass Museum, Sandwich, Massachusetts
Suwa Museum, Toyoda, Japan
The Toledo Museum of Art, Ohio
University of Michigan-Dearborn, Museum of Art
Victoria and Albert Museum, London
Wustum Museum of Fine Art, Racine, Wisconsin

Selected Bibliography

Bedula, Jane. *Glass from Ancient Craft to Contemporary Art: 1961–1992 and Beyond.* Morristown, New Jersey: The Morris Museum, 1992.

Brand, David, "In New Jersey, Capturing Nature in Glass." *Time Magazine,* February 8, 1988, p. 12.

Charleston, Robert J. *Masterpieces of Glass: A World History From The Corning Museum of Glass.* New York: Harry N. Abrams, Inc., 1990.

Cristalomancia: Contemporary Art in Glass. Monterrey, Mexico: Centro De Arte Vitro, 1992.

Dietz, Ulysses Grant. *Celebrating Diversity in Craft: The New Jersey Arts Annual.* Newark: The Newark Museum, 1995.

Ellis, William S. "Glass: Capturing the Dance of Light." *National Geographic,* vol. 184, no. 6, December 1993.

Heller, Douglas. *Paul Stankard.* New York: Heller Gallery, 1993.

Hollister, Paul. "Natural Wonders: The Lampwork of Paul J. Stankard." *American Craft,* February/March 1987.

The International Exhibition of Glass Kanazawa '92. Kanazawa, Japan: Kanazawa Chamber of Commerce and Industry, 1992.

Klein, Daniel. *Glass: A Contemporary Art.* New York: Rizzoli International Publications, Inc., 1989.

Lechaczynski, Serge. "Azur." *Verriales '92.* Biot, France: Galerie Internationale du Verre, 1992.

Morris, Jim. "Nature Reflected in Glass." *New Jersey Outdoors,* Fall 1992.

New Glass Review 13. Corning: The Corning Museum of Glass, 1992.

Paul J. Stankard: Poetry In Glass. Neenah, Wisconsin: Bergstrom-Mahler Museum, 1990.

Prism of Fantasy, From the Glass Collection of Hokkaido Museum of Modern Art. Hokkaido, Japan: Hokkaido Shumbun Press, 1990.

Spillman, Jane Shadel, and Susanne K. Frantz. *Masterpieces of American Glass.* New York: Crown Publishers, Inc., 1990.

Tomoko, Aoki. "Paul Stankard Talks About His Life and Work." *Glasswork,* July 1992, pp. 10–17.

Warmus, William. "Paul Stankard." *New Work Glass,* no. 37, Spring 1989.

Yoshimizu, Tsuneo. *Survey of Glass in the World.* Tokyo: Kyuryudo Art Publishing Co., Ltd., 1992.

Yood, James. "Flowers from a Flame." exh. cat. Marx Saunders Gallery, Chicago, 1995.